5 MINUTES
with the SAINTS

More Spiritual Nourishment for
Busy Teachers

edited by

Lou DelFra, C.S.C., *and* Ann Primus Berends
of the Alliance for Catholic Education
University of Notre Dame

AVE MARIA PRESS AVE Notre Dame, Indiana

Founded in 1865, Ave Maria Press is a ministry of the United States Province of Holy Cross.

www.avemariapress.com

Paperback: ISBN-13 978-1-59471-448-1

E-book: ISBN-13 978-1-59471-449-8

Cover image © imageBROKER/Alamy.

Cover and text design by Katherine Robinson.

Printed and bound in the United States of America.

Library of Congress Cataloging-in-Publication Data

Five minutes with the saints : more spiritual nourishment for busy teachers / edited by Lou DelFra, C.S.C., and Ann Primus Berends of the Alliance for Catholic Education, University of Notre Dame.

    pages cm

  Includes bibliographical references and index.

  ISBN 978-1-59471-448-1

  1. Catholic teachers–Prayers and devotions. 2. Education (Christian theology)–Meditations. 3. Christian saints–Quotations. I. DelFra, Lou, editor. II. Berends, Ann Primus, editor.

  BX2170.T43F58 2014

  242'.68--dc23

                            2014018890

provide much-needed spiritual nourishment for Catholic educators. Spending a few minutes a day with these reflections will result in many hours of spiritual growth and personal peace."

Diane Starkovich
Superintendent of Schools
Archdiocese of Atlanta

"After forty years in Catholic education, I was encouraged by three aspects of *5 Minutes with the Saints*: the variety of saints, from the well-known and -established such as Joseph and Paul, to those who were more contemporary; the stories of the saints dedicated to Catholic education that reaffirmed my belief in the communion of saints; and the reflections and personal stories of my fellow Catholic educators that became a springboard for my own prayer and contemplation."

Robert F. Siccone
Assistant Principal
Archbishop McCarthy High School
Southwest Ranches, FL

"*5 Minutes with the Saints* is a much-needed resource for Catholic school teachers who are challenged on all sides by the secular demands imposed on education today. If we, as Catholic educators and administrators, are to promote authentic Catholic identity in our schools, then we must be led and inspired by those who truly embrace what it means to teach as Jesus did.

5 Minutes with the Saints unites thought-provoking and uplifting quotations from the saints with anecdotes and insights from dedicated Catholic educators of our time. Whether you choose an entry a day, search for inspiration on a particular topic that is challenging you, or simply read the text straight through, *5 Minutes with the Saints* is a book for every faithful and faith-filled Catholic educator.

Maria Steen
Religion Department Chair and Campus Minister
Archbishop Chapelle High School
Metairie, LA

5 MINUTES
with the SAINTS

"*5 Minutes with the Saints* is a valuable resource, particularly for anyone working in Catholic education. Its simple format is especially useful for the busy teacher, allowing the reader to open to any page to find a brief reflection related to the life of a saint in light of the lived experiences of Catholic educators. A good Catholic school should help all its students to become saints; what better support can there be for teachers than this delightful collection that inspires them to share the life of such witnesses!"

Timothy J. McNiff
Superintendent of Schools
Archdiocese of New York

"These reflections on the words, wisdom, and lives of saints—many of whom were teachers—will inspire, encourage, challenge, and comfort Catholic educators. They remind us that teachers are the instruments of the God who called them to teach, and that Christ is and has always been the center of our educational mission."

Kathy Schoen
Director of Elementary Religious Education
Curriculum/Personnel
Archdiocese of St. Louis

"Another wonderful resource for our teachers and catechists. Following the format of *5 Minutes with Christ*, the reflections contained in *5 Minutes with the Saints*

CONTENTS

INTRODUCTION

In the sixth month the angel Gabriel was sent from God to a city in Galilee called Nazareth, to a virgin engaged to a man named Joseph; and the virgin's name was Mary. Gabriel said to her, "Greetings, favored one! The Lord is with you." But Mary was very perplexed at this statement, and kept pondering what kind of salutation this was. The angel said to her, "Do not be afraid, Mary; for you have found favor with God. And behold, you will conceive in your womb and bear a son, and you shall name Him Jesus." Mary said to the angel, "How can this be, since I am a virgin?" The angel answered and said to her, "The Holy Spirit will come upon you, and the power of the Most High will overshadow you; and for that reason the holy Child shall be called the Son of God. For nothing will be impossible with God." And Mary said . . .

Luke 1:26–38

Is there a more beautiful word for a human being to utter than the word *Yes?*

I used to teach language arts and so was always urging students to discover and use words that reflected the beauty of the people, places, and things they were describing. Words of vitality. Words of poetic vibrancy. Words that leapt off the page and brought their described realities to life.

If you teach science, is there any moment more delightful (and I know this must happen *all* the time) than when a student opens his or her mouth and out comes a word like *phosphorescence*? Or when a math student questions whether the most beautiful number is "*e* to the *i* pi power"? What reality could be described by such a marvelous phrase?

I remember sitting in social studies as a middle school student. As everyone around me learned about the American Revolutionary War, I sat writing the word *Ticonderoga* over and over again in the margins of my notebook—what a word!

Alphabet, *parabola*, *ferrocarril* (have you ever heard a fifth grader try a double trill in Spanish?), *onomatopoeia*. Our lives as teachers are filled—sometimes sparingly (especially after recess!) but always potentially—with words that are saturated with the beauty of the realities they are describing. Somehow, through the mysterious power of language, these words reflect that beauty back to us.

Yet, for all the beauty of the human vocabulary, an entirely new power of language that communicates the deepest reality of the human soul is revealed in the story of the recreation of the universe—at the annunciation. This encounter in the Gospel of Luke between the angel Gabriel and the Virgin Mary, in which she fully surrenders to the plan of God revealed by the angel, makes us stop and think: Can any human word, no matter how poetic in rhyme or grandeur, match the simple beauty, radical affirmation, and universe-changing power of the word Mary's soul uttered to Gabriel, so many centuries ago?

Yes.

Just for a moment, think about the times in your life when you have had to choose whether or not to use this word. Is there any moment more potentially creative, more potentially explosive, more life-affirming, more open to disappointment, more risky than a moment shared between two people that requires the use of that one simple word? A question is asked, exposing the vulnerability of one to another. A need is expressed. A desire made known.

"Will you help me?"

"Do you believe me?"

"Can you forgive me?"

"Do you love me?"

When such questions are posed, a period of charged silence—potential energy—gathers between the questioner and the one questioned, just as it did between Gabriel and Mary. In that silence, the mind races through imagined consequences. It weighs the costs and gains of assenting or withholding. The heart listens for echoes from its sometimes unplumbed depths as the demands of the question probe desires and fears, virtues and vulnerabilities. And, beneath and amidst all the commotion of mind and heart, the will attempts

to absorb it all. It wavers back and forth, now attracted, now hesitant, now horrified, now excited by the
possibilities.

And for a few tense moments, or days, or weeks, as
this inner dynamic runs its course, on the outside—in
the space between questioner and the one questioned,
between Gabriel and Mary—there is just silence. An
unknown outcome awaits.

In a home in Nazareth, Gabriel's invitation hangs in
the air. It's as if the whole universe is holding its breath.
And then, is there a reality more beautiful than the one
that next wells up from Mary's soul?

Surely you can recall times in your life when you
have allowed the little word *yes* to escape your lips. And
so you know well all the unintended consequences—
from the positively ecstatic to the utterly miserable—
that the utterance of this little word unleashes; all the
unforeseen, sometimes completely absurd, sometimes
downright painful, places this word will take you.

The annunciation consoles us here. Undoubtedly,
Mary knows all too well what we are experiencing. For
how little of her future was clear that night when Gabriel's invitation unfolded before her? Just think of all that
she could not possibly have discerned that evening as
the angel's invitation hung in the air. How would she
explain her yes to Joseph, or her parents, or her neighbors, who wondered at her swollen belly, knowing that
she and Joseph had not yet become husband and wife?

Perhaps you have had moments when you wondered how to explain yourself to others; perhaps the choice of your vocation of teaching was met with some surprise, or with predictions of financial demise, or early burnout. However discouraged you might have felt, your circumstances could not possibly have been more complicated than Mary's as she explained what had happened to Anne and Joachim, saints though they may have been.

And the drama only intensified from here. Surely Mary could not have foreseen, on that quiet night in Nazareth, that soon she would be hoisted onto the back of a pack mule in the middle of the night, panicked and pregnant, and whisked off to a foreign country in a scene that would make the whirlwind of our classrooms seem but a passing breeze.

Still, whether our yes was to the invitation to teach or (as it was with Mary) to something more momentous, what unexpected displacement this little word has unleashed in our lives.

As Mary's story unfolds quietly, as we glimpse it in the background of the gospels and tradition, it seems certain that the consequences of her yes only grew more complicated. From the exhilaration of the Magi or the wine stewards at Cana, affirming her yes; to the terror of Herod's murderous threats or the anxiety of losing her twelve-year-old for days in the Temple. Surely neither the peaks nor the valleys could have been foreseen by Mary the night of her initial assent. The joys and struggles that follow our yesses are never really known beforehand, are they? And perhaps this is best, for if they were, would it be any surprise if none of us ever said yes to anything at all?

At one startling point, Mary wishes to see her son, now grown and a religious teacher of some popularity. She sends word into the house where he is teaching, requesting his presence. Word is brought back to her that, when Jesus heard her request, he responded, "Who is my mother? Here are my mother and brothers" (Mt 12:48–49).

What did that feel like for the one who always said yes to him? How could she have known on that first night, Gabriel's invitation hovering before her, that her yes would expose her at times to such apparent rejection? Jesus was always off doing the incomprehensible, and so many days, she must have been barely hanging on. She was charged by the angel that night in Nazareth to care for him, yet he seemed in this moment, and so many others, to respond incoherently, to go off and do his own off-the-wall thing, not to need or appreciate what his mother was offering.

Perhaps this sounds like a certain someone, or someones, with whom you spend eight hours a day, five days a week?

What did Mary feel at perplexing times like this? Perhaps, in that moment outside that house, the already-skeptical and gossipy villagers relaying Jesus' words with a scowling laugh—"He said, 'Who is my mother?'"—she felt that she no longer understood what was being asked of her. That maybe after all, she didn't have what it took to keep up with her yes.

Perhaps, this day, and time and time again throughout her life, challenges crept in: *I didn't know it would be like this. I didn't know it would demand this much.* Perhaps (and I would never suggest this to any Christian readership other than an audience of teachers) there were days when the thought briefly crossed her mind: *I know I said yes to caring for him, but today he is driving me nuts, and I am ready to call down fire and brimstone upon his dear head!* (Just maybe, I am projecting some of my own experience in the classroom here.)

And yet, amidst all the perplexity and soul-testing challenges that constantly confronted Mary in the years of her son's public ministry, we must also acknowledge one thing more. For the gospels and tradition reveal one thing more at every turn and without fail. That somehow in the midst of all this unpredictable commotion and constant disorientation, amidst what could have only felt like days of little progress or even backward direction, for some reason—possibly that can only be explained by grace—one word kept welling up inside this woman, and maybe even in her own disbelief, one word kept escaping from her mouth—that most beautiful word, which first welled up in her soul in her home in Nazareth. *Yes.*

I'll trust. This will make sense at some point. From the beginning, this was God's initiative, not mine. So, yes. I will be there. I'll be with him. Again and again and again. Even to what seemed at the time to be the bitter end. Her son—the fruit of her yes—is on the road to Calvary, the cross laid heavy across his shoulder. Are we so surprised to find her even here, at his life's end, at this gruesome point? Emerging from the crowd, a lifetime of daily yesses to all the twists and turns, which were forged in her courage and faithfulness that knew no bounds, she silently demands that Jesus meet her gaze. And when at last he does, Mary's tear-streaked face is miraculously speaking the one word that summed up her entire life. And Jesus' shoulders heave the cross upward as he, too, is filled with only yes.

This is the woman—the saint—whom we honor with the title Queen of Saints. By their words, witness, and works, saints—like the saints who inspired the reflections of the educators in this book—are educators par excellence. They teach us what it means to be a disciple of Christ.

Mary stands first among them. What does she teach us about discipleship? From what we have said above, we learn from her that to be a disciple of Christ is not to be someone graced with a clear and certain vision of our future and all the consequences of our yesses.

Mary, it seems, was not afforded this. To be a disciple of Christ is not to be blessed with daily tasks of predictable constancy, always convenient (or even sane) requests, or uninterrupted peace of mind. To be a disciple of Christ is not even to lay our well-worked heads and bodies to sleep each night in the sure and certain knowledge that today has been a success. No reading of Mary's life could lead us to surmise that this is how her evenings always ended.

Surely Christian joy was the deepest reality of Mary's life. Yet just as surely, this joy was not immediately available at every moment and must at times have seemed completely out of grasp or even lost. And even as any "dark nights of the soul" wore on, just as surely dawn would break again in Nazareth each morning. Mary would rub the sleep from her eyes. Possibly in those first moments of wakefulness, her mind would begin to race, wondering what more could possibly unfold this day. And her heart some mornings would feel a pang of worry or anxiety or a gasp of fatigue at what uncertain surprises and demands her yes would reveal today.

Yet, perhaps, on those mornings, the memory of the annunciation would return—that quiet, still night when Gabriel appeared and offered his invitation "Will you?"—and Mary would come to recognize yet again the secret of all the saints: *It was not only me who answered that evening. I heard the invitation, sat in the silence, and opened myself as best I could, as much as grace would allow, to the will of God. And then I remember God's voice lifted mine, and together we voiced that most beautiful word*—Yes.

Here is one lesson that Mary and all the saints after her teach us: our lives and the invitation to discipleship that lies at their core are God's from beginning to end. As we have been called to educate, to care for students, to witness the love of God to them, in the midst of all the demands and sacrifices, surprises and joys of that call, we are called first and foremost to trust that God is with us. All is unfolding in God's plan. The saints exhort us to believe this totally. When we do, there can be only *yes*.

This book is a collection of reflections on the lives or sayings of several saints, many of whom were either educators themselves or founded communities dedicated to education. By their words, witness, and works, these saints teach and encourage us to open our lives as educators—with a constant, persevering, and joyous yes!—to the ways God is transforming us into instruments of grace for our students and colleagues. These reflections are written by a faith-filled community of educators in the University of Notre Dame's Alliance for Catholic Education (ACE)—teachers, principals, administrators, and members of the ACE academic and pastoral team who direct the formation of teachers and principals. We hope these daily reflections provide spiritual nourishment for any educator striving to open themselves to God's wondrous designs in the midst of the busyness of the school day.

Our lives, the lives of our students, and the lives of the members of our school communities are not unfolding according to our plans; they are unfolding according to God's plan. Let us open ourselves with Mary and the Communion of Saints so that God's voice might renew within us that most beautiful word.

Fr. Lou DelFra, C.S.C.
Alliance for Catholic Education (ACE)
University of Notre Dame, Notre Dame, Indiana

REFLECTIONS

Saints are people before they are saints, and they may be made of every sort or kind of person; and most of us will choose between these different types according to our different tastes.

A saint may be any kind of person, with an additional quality that is at once unique and universal. We might even say that the one thing that separates a saint from ordinary people is his or her readiness to be one with ordinary people. In this sense the word ordinary must be understood in its native and noble meaning, which is connected with the word order. A saint is long past any desire for distinction; a saint is only the sort of superior person who has never been a superior person.

G. K. Chesterton

Saint Albert the Great

The Importance of Questions

The aim of natural science is not simply to accept the statements of others, but to investigate the causes that are at work in nature.

A colleague and friend of mine who researches science education has been in hundreds of classrooms and talked with hundreds of students. I'll never forget one interview he shared with me of a young boy who was asked to describe his science class. The boy bemoaned, "Science class is a bunch of answers to questions I never asked."

As teachers, we often love our subject so much that we can't wait to impart our knowledge to our students. And woe to the courageous student who interrupts our lecture to ask "Why?" or "How do we know this is true?" Can't they just accept the wisdom we have offered?

We know better, of course. Good science teachers eschew telling students what to believe, instead challenging them to ask questions, seek answers, and construct their own meaning about God's creation.

Fortunately, the Church gives us examples of those strong in the faith, like Albert the Great, who constantly questioned and explored the world around them. Long before Albert was a bishop or a Doctor of the Church, he was much like our students (and hopefully

us)—curious about the world and full of questions.
Albert learned about the world around him not just
from books but by actually observing and experiment-
ing with nature. He saw God in both the mystery of
and the answers to the questions that intrigued him.

Albert's philosophy is instructive not just for sci-
entists but for all teachers. If investigation is an aim of
natural science, then our teaching must invite students
to question nature and creation, to feed their innate
curiosity, and yes, at times, even to question what we
teach.

Matt Kloser
Center for STEM Education
University of Notre Dame
Notre Dame, Indiana

Saint Alberto Hurtado

Christ is without a home! Shouldn't we want to give him one, those of us who have the joy of a comfortable home, plenty of good food, the means to educate and assure the future of our children? "What you do to the least of me, you do to me," Jesus said.

Alberto Hurtado Cruchaga, affectionately remembered throughout his home country of Chile simply as "Padre Hurtado," is a Jesuit saint whose radical love for and commitment to children on the margins of society continue to serve as a powerful model for all educators.

When Alberto was four years old, his father died and his once-comfortable family was cast into poverty. His mother was forced to pass her two young sons from relative to relative as she struggled to pay her family's debts. In the midst of the vulnerability that had come to define the contours of young Alberto's life, he received a scholarship that enabled him to attend San Ignacio al Bosque, a prestigious Jesuit school for boys in Santiago. Through Alberto's teachers and mentors, God kindled within the young man the flame of his vocation, not only to the Jesuit priesthood but also to a life of humble solidarity with those in poverty, especially children.

5

As a Jesuit, Alberto collaborated with local women
to found Hogar de Cristo ("Christ's Home"), a network
of shelters, hospices, and educational centers for economically marginalized men, women, and children
throughout Chile. He also purchased what would
become an iconic symbol of his ministry: a green
pickup truck, which he would use to bring homeless
children to Hogar de Cristo. He called the children his
patroncitos (his "little bosses"), signifying by this title
their dignity and his deeply felt duty to serve their
needs.

Because of his refusal to ignore children on the
margins, the work of Saint Alberto Hurtado grew into
one of Chile's largest and most comprehensive social
service organizations. May we as educators embrace a
preferential option for our most economically, cogni-
tively, and socially marginalized students. May we, like
Padre Hurtado, dare to call them our *patroncitos*—our
little bosses.

Susan Bigelow Reynolds
Department of Theology and Education
Boston College Graduate Program
Boston, Massachusetts

Saint Alberto Hurtado

In order to teach, it is enough to know something. But to educate, one must be something. True education consists of giving oneself as a living model, an authentic lesson.

"Do you get mad when we call you *gringo*?"

Every so often my students in Chile ask me this question. It's a fair one; *gringo* often has a pejorative meaning for English-speaking foreigners. As an English teacher, I appreciate their attention to words and their meanings. My response, however, is always the same: "Not at all, it's who I am!"

My ability to teach in Chile is not based on a wealth of experience of South American culture or a mastery of Spanish—far from it. Rather, as Alberto Hurtado suggests, it is based on who I am as a person. My "gringo-ness," so to speak, allows me to share and teach American culture in a way that enriches both my students and me.

Every day in the classroom, I am acutely aware of how different I look, sound, and act compared to the people around me. But these differences are a tremendous blessing. I am able to teach my students English not by dry transmission or rote memorization but by living among them, speaking with them, and just

7

being an American in and out of the classroom. As a result, my lessons are more authentic, my students are more engaged, and the language becomes much more practical.

As an American teacher in Santiago, I have learned to educate the entire person by following the advice of St. Alberto Hurtado: by giving myself as a living model—*gringo* as it may be! This is who I am, and it's how I teach. Today in our teaching and learning, let's concern ourselves less with what we know than with who we are. Let's give our whole selves as living models to our students and communities, just as Christ gave himself as a model to us.

Dan Faas
Saint George's College
Santiago, Chile

SAINT ALOYSIUS GONZAGA

A POWERFUL HUMILITY

*It is better to be the child of God than king of
the whole world.*

By his life, Aloysius Gonzaga lived these words faith-
fully. Born the oldest son of an Italian aristocrat,
he was destined for titles, privilege, and power. Against
the will and expectations of his father and family, however, Aloysius renounced his right to inheritance and
status and became a missionary. He chose a life of
service and purity, entering the Society of Jesus at age
seventeen.

Known for his strong inner spiritual life, Aloysius
gave this life powerful expression through his brave
and unconquerable compassion, working with vic-
tims of the plague and eventually dying from it at age
twenty-four. This young man was a beautiful example
of what we are all called to be, first and foremost: children of God.

This call can present conflicting thoughts and
expectations for educators. The world perceives success in terms of honors, acceptance into prestigious
universities, or the security of high-paying jobs. Do
we allow ourselves at times to be discouraged by these
seductive ideals that can seem so far from our daily

9

lives? Or do we recognize and appreciate the humility we have been called to exhibit in our classrooms?

We cannot expect our students to desire humility and lives of service without modeling it ourselves. At the same time, we do well to remember that while teaching is a service and the classroom is a place of humility, the profession also carries great power. May we never lose sight of that.

Read the quotation from St. Aloysius Gonzaga again. Is this not exactly the model of Christ's life? Who more than Jesus could have ruled this world justly and rightly? And yet he chose a humble and simple life—the life of a servant, the life of a teacher. At his death on the cross, his cry was for his "Abba."

Today let us try to forget the expectations of our world and simply be children of God.

Maureen Coulton
Holy Names Academy
Seattle, Washington

Saint Alphonsus Ligouri

The past is no longer yours; the future is not yet in your power. You have only the present wherein to do good.

Before I started teaching, I knew it would be a challenge; this seemed inherently obvious. What surprised me was where the challenges emerged. The biggest trials I faced each day had less to do with things I could control—like lesson plans—and much more to do with matters completely out of my control—students who started the school year lagging behind their peers, the bureaucratic boundaries they faced, and the broken homes from which they came. These disadvantages seemed to oppress my students and plague my classroom.

Regardless of my actions, I could not eliminate these obstacles. The frustration I felt mixed bitterly with anxiety as I took in everything that was working against my students. How could they possibly reach their potential under these circumstances? Why should success require so much extra work for them? Yet, in the face of what were at times impossible odds and with more than just occasional setbacks, these students showed up at school every morning. Their perseverance was a daily inspiration. The burdens of tomorrow and yesterday faded behind the brightness of hope in the light of each new day.

This is what God has given to us and to our students: today.

We need to recognize the present as just this: a present—one that has been given to us by God and one that we have the opportunity to use. Each day presents us with the choice of how we will use it.

May God take our frustrations from yesterday and our fears for tomorrow to help us recognize the beauty of today and grant us the strength to be good stewards of this gift—for our students and for God's glory.

Garrett Mandeville
Our Lady of Perpetual Help
New Orleans, Louisiana

Saint Ambrose

In the Gospel, we are taught to have faith and not draw back from doing those things which are above our human strength. Hope is incentive to labor.

As governor of a territory in northern Italy, Ambrose was sent to broker a peace between two groups feuding over the election of the next bishop of Milan. He so impressed the rival groups that they unanimously demanded that he become the bishop. There were just a few problems: He wasn't a priest. He had never studied theology. And he hadn't even been baptized yet.

The emperor, however, accepted the will of the crowd and, in just one week, Ambrose was baptized, ordained, and consecrated as the bishop of Milan. Seventeen centuries later, we celebrate him as a Doctor of the Church, a holy hero whose teaching and understanding of God have shaped the faith ever since that remarkable, whirlwind week.

Perhaps Ambrose's experience of being thrust into leadership led to his prayer. Hope gave him reason to strive, and the hope we find in the gospel likewise gives us the strength to do work that seems otherwise impossible.

Saint Ambrose Catholic School in Tucson, Arizona, is a Notre Dame ACE Academy where children and teachers wear T-shirts that read, "Whatever it takes IS what it takes." This motto reflects the same bold faith and courageous hope that inspired Ambrose's own leap of faith centuries ago. For the teachers at Saint Ambrose, sometimes it seems that the gospel demands an impossible task—to provide a Catholic education of the highest quality to children in a community crippled by poverty. However, that same gospel, the living Word of God, offers the strength, zeal, and tenacity needed to do whatever it takes to put each child on the path to college and heaven.

This simple mantra—"Whatever it takes"—reminds us of the promise of Ambrose's prayer: that if we act in ways that spread the hope of the gospel every day, not only will we be able to accomplish feats above our human strength, but we will also inspire others to do the same.

Christian Dallavis
ACE Leadership Programs
University of Notre Dame
Notre Dame, Indiana

Saint André Bessette

*When I first came to the college, I was shown
to the door . . . and I remained there for forty
years!*

I am sending you a saint." These were the words
of Father Andre Provencal, the parish priest who
wrote to the Holy Cross brothers, pleading with them
to accept young André Bessette—a small, sickly, and
illiterate orphan—into the religious life. Young André
was by all means desperate: he was too weak to hold
a steady job, unable to read or write, and poor, with
seemingly little to offer the world. Even the brothers
were not quite sure what to do with him, reluctantly
installing him as a doorkeeper at the College of Notre
Dame in Montreal.

From his position as porter, Brother André surprised everyone. His devotion to St. Joseph attracted
large crowds, who came to see him for hospitality, healing, and consolation. Desiring to build a shrine to St.
Joseph but lacking the funds, the young man began collecting nickels and praying fervently. Against all odds,
a grand basilica, St. Joseph's Oratory, was completed
after André's death in 1937. For all of his small works of
mercy and service and the unexpected miracles attributed to him, he was canonized on October 17, 2010, by

Pope Benedict XVI, becoming the Congregation of Holy Cross's first saint.

Perhaps you have a little André who comes to your classroom door each morning—weak, academically challenged, or sad. Perhaps you, the teacher, are not quite sure what to do with him or her. No doubt you are overworked and slightly overwhelmed by the challenge of meeting the individual needs of your students, as well as preoccupied with the many demands of your profession.

As teachers, through our sustained efforts we experience the graces of our vocation in the unexpected miracles that come from the young saints-in-the-making entrusted to our care. We watch them experience unexpected joy in perseverance, learn lessons of patience and humility, and grow in their understanding of God. These moments are truly miracles—unfolding in the most unexpected people—if we take the opportunity to notice them.

Who are the "doorkeepers" in your school or classroom? Be open today to the experience of unexpected miracles in your students and watch your own faith increase by their surprisingly graceful examples.

Molly W. Carlin
Queen of Angels Catholic School
Roswell, Georgia

Saint André Bessette

*It is with the smallest brushes that the artist
paints the most exquisitely beautiful pictures.*

As rector of a women's hall at the University of Notre Dame, I have the opportunity to share life with undergraduate women every day. I pray with them at Mass. I celebrate with them when they pass a test, cry with them when they lose a parent to cancer, and listen as they discern their future. This privilege humbles me daily.

As I listen, I'm especially struck by how often conversion happens in the smallest experiences. God doesn't change these young women through large crises or get their attention with a booming voice. Rather, God uses "small brushes": a class they are taking, a conversation that moves them to explore majors they never knew existed, a week of immersion in the culture of Appalachia.

I think of "Nicole," who was a sophomore my first year as rector. She was pre-med and a leader in almost every club on campus. Her plan was to pursue a high-profile medical profession after graduation, but one small experience led her in a different direction. Nicole went on a service trip to the "hollers" of West Virginia during fall break. After returning to campus, she stopped by my room one evening as I was making dinner. While I chopped veggies, she sat at my kitchen table and explained to me that through the week she had realized that she wanted her life to be one of service. She wanted to be a doctor who made her life about meeting the needs of the poor.

I cherish this memory, which confirms for me that the Lord uses little brushes to create and shade us. While it's easy to focus on the big conversion events of life, my students remind me not to miss the daily routines in which God speaks. In the words of Brother André—the man who became a saint through the simple occupation of doorkeeper—I hear a challenge to see and cherish God's transforming presence in the simple things. Today, may we open our doors to these small moments of conversion where God is painting the masterpieces of our lives.

Margaret Morgan
Howard Hall
University of Notre Dame
Notre Dame, Indiana

SAINT ANGELA MERICI

INSPIRED SURPRISES

Have hope and firm faith in God, for he will help you in everything. Act, move, believe, strive, hope, cry out to him with all your heart, for without doubt you will see marvelous things, if you direct everything to the praise and glory of his Majesty and the good of souls.

Dread hung over me as heavily as the Brownsville humidity during my first semester of teaching. When it struck early in the morning, the dread felt like a sharp stab from a needle; as the day progressed, it settled into a low, throbbing pain that lingered until the bell rang at the end of the day. The act of teaching wasn't the issue. It was the threat of surprise.

There were so many ways the day could go wrong. What if I finish the lesson early? What if the lesson flops and my students don't understand anything I tell them? What if the technology doesn't work? What about the problems I can't foresee? The fact that I could never prepare enough was the hardest thing to overcome.

As the months went by, I began to realize that surprise is part of the job. I also began to see that the days of mayhem and catastrophe were vastly outnumbered by the days of peace. There were even a few days when surprise turned to success, though I didn't always recognize it at the time.

One day in a desperate attempt to teach my freshmen about different climate regions, I made up a stupid jingle about prairies using the melody from a Justin Bieber song. The jingle was not successful in teaching my students about prairies, but it did bring together and energize the class. Stupid jingles—a surprise inspiration—became my tool for breaking tension and easing frustration when class wasn't going well.

That experience taught me that lesson plans are more like trampolines than shields and that each day will bring something I don't expect. We teachers can trust that God will help us in everything—even surprise.

Vickey McBride
Saint Martin de Porres High School
Cleveland, Ohio

Saints Anne and Joachim

Preparing the Gifts to Come

Legend and Church tradition tell the story of a childless couple visited by an angel, who promised them that they would soon have a child. The mother-to-be vowed to dedicate this child to God, and thus Anne and Joachim became the parents of Mary of Nazareth, who would in turn become the mother of Jesus.

At the end of every school year, our students walk out of the classroom one final time. While many will return in the fall, graduation, transfers, and a host of other circumstances mean that we have seen some of these children for the last time. We wonder what will come next for them. What marks will they make on the world, and how will the world make its mark on them?

Teaching is, after all, an act of faith. Through education, God gives our students the opportunity to develop their gifts; as teachers, we are privileged to play a central role in that formation. Some days feel like huge breakthroughs, and other days feel like nothing special. Yet somehow we know that God is using us to prepare our students for the work God will one day ask them to do. If only we could know! Wouldn't that help us as educators? If we could know that this student will one day be a journalist, this one a nurse, this one a priest, this one a teacher?

Anne and Joachim inspire us in this uncertainty. As Mary's first teachers, this holy couple simply did their best to raise their daughter, without knowing that she would be the vessel by which God would enter the world. Something about Mary's upbringing—probably a mix of the intentional and the providential in her parents' words and actions—prepared her to say yes to Gabriel. And the world was, after that, never again the same.

May God remind us of how blessed we are to influence our students' formation. May God guide us in doing the best we can in the days we have with them, trusting that their lives will be full of opportunities to make God known, loved, and served in our world.

Meghann Robinson Kirzeder
St. Ann Catholic School
Nashville, Tennessee

Saint Augustine of Hippo

But you sent down your help from above, and rescued my soul from the depths of this darkness because my mother [St. Monica], your faithful servant, wept to you for me, shedding more tears for my spiritual death than other mothers shed for the bodily death of a son.

Augustine of Hippo is known for many things, including his wild youth. He dabbled in just about everything we hope that our students will not! That he became such an important figure in the Church and an inspirational writer is due to the Holy Spirit working through the unceasing prayer and support of Augustine's mother, St. Monica. The patron saint of mothers can also serve as an example for teachers. She remained steadfast in the belief that God had a special vocation for her son and never abandoned her faith in God's power and mercy to bring Augustine back to him.

As educators, it is often difficult to see some of our students as special instruments of God. There are those who refuse to listen, seem disinterested in learning, and worry us with other behaviors in and outside of school. It's easy to forget that these students are often most in need of our prayers and loving service.

23

We cannot know what they are capable of—only God knows. So we must be their St. Monica.

In time, Augustine realized that all hearts are restless until they rest in God. Not all of our students will have the powerful conversion of heart that Augustine had, but we can hold him as a reminder of the great works that God does through those who may seem least capable. Our hearts will also remain restless if we do not believe in, pray for, and do our best for the "least" among our students. Like St. Monica, we are instruments of God, and our work may make all the difference in our students' struggles to become who God wants them to be.

Laura Wolohan
Father Ryan High School
Nashville, Tennessee

Saint Augustine of Hippo

*Love, and do what you will. If you keep silence,
do it out of love. If you cry out, do it out of love.
If you refrain from punishing, do it out of love.*

The first sentence of this quotation from Augustine was my classroom motto in my first year as a middle school teacher. A product of an Augustinian high school, I wanted to share my love of Augustine's theology and spirituality with my students. I admittedly had some doubts about how my sixth graders, who were sometimes overenergetic and constantly testing boundaries, would interpret Augustine's words. Yet on day one I went ahead and hung the laminated quotation above the whiteboard, front and center.

As the first day came to a close, I introduced the quotation as our class motto for the year and asked the students to interpret it. The first response was not quite right: "So if I tell my mom I love her every day, I can do whatever I want?" But the second response showed that Augustine's insight resonated with my sixth graders, as it has with countless people throughout the centuries: "If we make sure love is at the center of everything we do, we will live a good life and go to heaven. If we are loving and acting out of love, then we're living like Jesus. It's simple."

In the whirlwind of that first day of teaching, it struck me: It is pretty simple, isn't it? We are to be Christ in the classroom, loving our kids as Christ does. When we instruct, we need to do it out of love. When we discipline, we need to do it out of love. When we meet with parents, we need to do it out of love. Love deepens and transforms all our efforts in the classroom into an encounter with God, who is Love.

Luckily, if we ever lose our focus, our students have a way of reminding us of this simple truth—even on day one.

Patrick Kirkland
St. Frances Cabrini Catholic School
Savannah, Georgia

BLESSED BASIL MOREAU

*The art of Christian education is bringing
the young to wholeness in the person of Jesus
Christ.*

No single day in the school year is more exciting than that very first encounter with a new
class. Looking out on the unfamiliar faces, we see in
the expressions the mystery of knowledge not yet
exchanged and the friendships not yet formed.

This past summer, I was privileged to visit Florence,
where I gazed for the first time upon Michelangelo's
David. The experience made me wonder what it must
have been like for that master craftsman to imagine a
grace-filled form hidden within a gigantic, unformed
block of marble. To recognize and bring to light the hidden possibility, the potential of such sheer and utter
beauty, is the gift of the artist.

For Basil Moreau, this is the vocation of the teacher:
To sense the mystery at hand and to coax out of the
somewhat inchoate the loveliness and grace that lies
hidden. Teaching requires a radical act of imagination
to accomplish this. One must trust that within each
student "there lies the dearest freshness deep down
things" (G.M. Hopkins). And one must be utterly

relentless in engaging our students in a personal and even sacramental encounter.

The invitation to "wholeness in the person of Jesus Christ" is an invitation to full human flourishing; *wholeness* becomes *holiness*. It is an invitation to come to know and experience fully the freedom and joy of the children of God.

Fr. Tim Scully, C.S.C.
Institute for Educational Initiatives
Alliance for Catholic Education
University of Notre Dame
Notre Dame, Indiana

SAINT BENEDICT OF NURSIA

Let [the leader] be discreet and moderate, bearing in mind the discretion of holy Jacob, who said, "If I cause my flocks to be overdriven, they will all die in one day." Taking this, then, and other examples of discretion, the mother of virtues, let [the leader] so temper all things that the strong may have something to strive after, and the weak may have nothing to fear.

The final phrase of this advice from Benedict is the epitome of the challenge and call to school leadership. Books could be written about the goals of education, about outcomes, about processes, about virtues—but in the end, our charge as educational leaders is to help all students do their best, so that in all things God may be glorified.

From a pedagogical perspective, this means challenging each student in the ways that best suit his or her particular abilities. From a leadership perspective, it means leveraging the gifts around us to ensure that achievements within our schools are maximized. In the end, it is not about a mere equity for all in which every share is the same; it is about fairness for all in which those for whom we are responsible receive what they need and produce at the full level of their potential.

As a principal, I use Benedict's exhortation as an anchor point for each of our teachers, both as a method to encourage personal responsibility and development and as a way to lower the barriers that prevent teachers from acknowledging imperfection or inadequacy. Through it all, I point out one important fact about Benedict's challenge: When he wrote these words, those he referred to were members of a monastery. The call, therefore, is not to autonomous individuals but to individuals living in community—what an image for a school faculty or a classroom of learners!

In short, the goal to which Benedict urges us is not merely personal fulfillment but personal responsibility to a community. This shared mission can ensure that all who encounter our schools will come to know that our bars are set high but also that we are full of compassion—that "the strong have something to strive for, and the weak have nothing to fear."

Matthew Vereecke
Monte Cassino School
Tulsa, Oklahoma

Saint Benedict of Nursia

Listen . . . and incline the ear of your heart.

During my first few weeks of teaching, I kept losing my voice by the time Friday rolled around. My habit of talking—a lot—and then imploring students to listen was the perfect recipe for losing my voice, not to mention teaching my students to associate listening with boredom! We tell our students to listen so very often, but how often do we take our own advice?

It's one thing simply to listen to what someone is saying. We listen to students' questions so that we can answer them. Or we listen to a player in the huddle telling us there are too many players on the court so that we can avoid a penalty. But listening with "the ear of your heart," as Benedict counsels, requires us to go deeper.

The founder of Western contemplative monastic life encourages us to join actively with the speaker in what he or she is saying. And sometimes when we do, we can hear the most important things even from the people we're sick of hearing from, like the parent who just won't stop hassling us about her son and his poor performance. When we listen to her with the ear of our hearts, we may hear that the teacher at her son's last school told him that he couldn't learn and would just be another statistic and that she put everything she had into trusting that our school would help him realize the great potential she saw in him. Perhaps our hearts will hear that she is hassling us about helping him for the same reason we've been hassling him about doing his work—belief that he can do it.

As teachers, we often want to have eyes in the back of our heads. Benedict reminds us that it is just as important to have ears in our hearts. May we not forget to listen with our hearts to all whose lives we have been invited to share.

Alec Torigian
Most Pure Heart of Mary
Mobile, Alabama

SAINT BERNADETTE SOUBIROUS

VITA, DULCEDO, ET SPES

*Dearest Mother, how happy was my soul those
heavenly moments when I gazed upon you.
How I love to remember those sweet moments
spent in your presence, your eyes filled with
kindness and mercy for us. Yes, dear Mother,
your heart is so full of love for us that you
came down to earth to appear to a poor, weak
child and convey certain tidings to her despite
her great unworthiness.*

When I visit a grotto of Our Lady, which often
includes a statue of Bernadette kneeling in
prayer before her, I find myself saying to the young
saint, "Please pray with me to our Lady." I like to pray
with Bernadette rather than *through* her. For me, this
perspective does not lessen her ability to intercede;
rather, it elevates her virtue of faith. Bernadette selflessly invites my gaze upward. Her example gives me
the comfort and support I need to spend time in prayer
with our Blessed Mother.

Perhaps you are familiar with her story. Marie-Ber-
narde Soubirous was only fourteen when the Blessed
Mother appeared to her as she gathered firewood near
the cave in Massabielle, France. Over time, the Blessed
Virgin Mary graced Bernadette with eighteen appari-
tions and gave her certain messages to share with the

faithful. Bernadette delivered Mary's words to skeptics and supporters alike.

As educators, we have chosen a vocation with its own share of skeptics and supporters. Therefore, we need to model the same faith for our students that Bernadette displayed in our Blessed Mother. Through us, our students must hear Our Lady's invitation to place themselves at her feet, open in prayer, ready to receive her grace. In a sense, as teachers we must become like Bernadette, living examples of companions in prayer so as to deepen our students' faith.

In my own prayer life, I am grateful that I can use this example of Bernadette as I devote my prayer time through Mary. I look for ways to create my own contemplative grotto so that I may sit at the feet of Mary and ask for her grace to carry on the message that there is great "life, sweetness, and hope" (*vita, dulcedo, et spes*) in Catholic education.

Michael Kelleher
Saint Bernadette Catholic School
Springfield, Virginia

SAINT CATHERINE OF SIENA

About your desire, if it is of God, then God will provide the way and means such as you never could have imagined. Leave it all to him, let go of yourself, lose yourself in the cross and you will find yourself perfectly.

If Catherine of Siena lived today, I could see her having a Facebook page and Twitter account. She would likely use these mediums for communicating her love of God and desires for the good of humanity and through both would have lots of followers.

Alas, fourteenth-century Italy had no Facebook and no Twitter, but Catherine had lots of followers. And without modern-day means to communicate with them, Catherine took to letter writing. Dictating to one of her many disciples, she wrote to popes, to royalty, to nobles, and to simpler folks. One of her correspondents was Sister Daniella, a nun struggling with a desire to go off to Rome in service to the Church rather than remain cloistered in her convent.

To Sister Daniella, Catherine wrote: "About your desire, if it is of God, then God will provide the way and means such as you never could have imagined. Leave it all to him, let go of yourself, lose yourself in the cross and you will find yourself perfectly." This message is profoundly relevant in any age.

Every teacher engages in questioning: Should I take on additional responsibilities such as starting a new club or chairing a committee? Should I pursue further studies to improve my classroom practice? Do I switch grade levels or teach different subjects to fulfill a school need? Catherine's words advise us all to look to God. If something is of God, then God will show the way and provide the means to make it happen.

As we live this day, may we bring before God questions of discernment, and may we heed the advice of Catherine and trust that God will show the way. Let us "leave it all to him."

Sr. Gail Mayotte, S.A.S.V.
ACE Service through Teaching
University of Notre Dame
Notre Dame, Indiana

Saint Catherine of Siena

Nothing great is ever achieved without much enduring.

This quote by Catherine of Siena makes me think of my former student, "Devin," who has special needs. He does not verbally speak other than when asked to read aloud. He does, however, communicate through body language. Devin has the biggest smile a child could wear. His eyes twinkle. He exudes joy. He is quiet. He is respectful. He keeps his hands by his sides and nods his head yes and no when asked questions. When he needs a hug, he backs up into you and snuggles his head down to his chest.

Devin is an excellent reader. He reads for hours with his grandmother; his tutor; and me, his teacher. But even with all of this one-on-one attention, Devin would not be the student he is without his individual endurance. He is a hard worker. He is determined. He is persistent.

When I'm having a tough day, when a lesson plan I spent hours prepping flops, when I'm tired, when a parent-teacher conference does not go well, I think of

Devin. I am inspired to endure the way he endures. He reminds me that "nothing great is ever achieved without much enduring."

In your reflection today, ask yourself: What have I witnessed a student achieve through endurance? What have I achieved through endurance? And where must I continue to endure, as Catherine did, in order to achieve?

May God help us endure today—for our students, our coworkers, ourselves, and Him.

Elizabeth Stowe Fennell
Resurrection Catholic Elementary School
Pascagoula, Mississippi

Venerable Catherine McAuley

In correcting and punishing your pupils, imitate a good mother, avoiding both extreme laxity and extreme severity; endeavoring to combine prudence with impartiality, justice, and equity.

David" was an intelligent, capable freshman who loved causing trouble far more than he enjoyed school. In my English classroom, he knew just how to push my buttons. He mocked my enthusiasm openly in class. He was rude to his classmates. He made it very clear that he couldn't care less about reading, writing, or prayer.

One of the reasons I was attracted to teaching was that it would encourage me to be God's instrument—one who shared God's love even with those who weren't easy to love. Well, "Ask and it shall be given to you!" David was not easy for me to love.

One Monday, as I walked around the room checking grammar homework, I saw David take my teacher guide off my desk and copy answers into his workbook. I took David's grammar book away and, for the rest of the week, kept assigning workbook practice while conveniently "forgetting" to return his book. I was fed up with David's infractions, and I knew he was in need of correction, but my method was completely unfair.

Thursday after school, David's mom stopped me in the hallway outside my classroom. She was angry, but she spoke her message clearly: "Treat my son justly." I immediately thought of my own mother, one of my best teachers. My mom is famous in our family for her gentle, admonishing catchphrase: "That's somebody's son!" Whenever she found her children complaining about someone—even a Notre Dame quarterback— she reminded us that that person is somebody's son or daughter.

Catherine McAuley's words invite us to care for our students a "third way"—the parent way that, like a good mother, looks at children with eyes of justice and compassion.

Today, may we approach each of our students the parent way, honoring them, challenging them, and encouraging them to become their best.

Sarah Perkins
McGill-Toolen Catholic High School
Mobile, Alabama

Servant of God Dorothy Day

I thought again, the only answer in this life,
to the loneliness we are all bound to feel, is
community.

Throughout my experiences as a teacher, an administrator, and a parent, I've found Dorothy Day's words fitting. She says that the only solution to overcoming loneliness is love and that love comes from community. With the support of community, we can more easily see the presence of God.

As a teacher, I often felt alone when overwhelmed with responsibilities, activities, and grading. Repeatedly, small and simple interactions with others—a phone call with a family member or a friend, a take-out dinner with a colleague during a grading marathon—made the demands seem less challenging, less overwhelming, and less isolating.

As a principal, I remember feeling cut off from the camaraderie the staff shared or abandoned when I felt attacked or unappreciated. Again, my communities of fellow administrators, family, and friends were tremendous sources of strength. Conversations with those who played the same role reminded me that others face similar challenges. Interactions with family and friends were life-giving and reassuring.

As a stay-at-home parent, I feel that same loneliness when I struggle to find patience with my children, when I long for adult interaction, or when I endure the strain of sleeplessness. It is as if I am the only one who worries that I won't be able to adequately prepare my children for life. Not surprisingly, community takes away that loneliness and insecurity. Other parents, family, and friends offer camaraderie, reassurance, and understanding.

In all aspects of our lives, community lightens our loads and lifts us from the darkness of loneliness to the light of Christ, who is the presence of God with us. Community provides the support we need to perform the sacred work to which we are called.

Kathleen McCann Ojeda
Christ the Redeemer Parish
Sterling, Virginia

SAINT ELIZABETH ANN SETON

DAILY GARDENING

Give some time every day, if it is only half an hour, to devotional reading, which is as necessary to the well-ordering of the mind as the hand of the gardener is to prevent the weeds from destroying your favorite plants.

When I was a child, my mother would often ask me to help with the weeding in her garden. Begrudgingly, I performed the mundane and tedious task that resulted in sore muscles, grass-stained clothing, and bug bites. *Why do we have to do this every day? Surely there's an easier way. Why can't Mom's plants just cohabitate with the weeds?*

Even though my assistance was inconsistent, Mom made it a point to care for her garden on a daily basis, and it showed. Mom's dedication taught me that for a garden to be beautiful, it must be tended to every day. Could there have been any better preparation for the vocation of teaching? Like a garden, or like our students, our minds need constant attention and care. In order to remain focused, we must dedicate time for daily devotional reading and reflection.

As I begin each day, I have every intention of spending some quiet time with God. In my work at a Catholic high school, however, my daily agenda is quickly filled with a hundred "more urgent" tasks. *I need to return a parent's phone call. I have to meet with a family. There is an upcoming event that requires planning.*

If we allow ourselves to become consumed with duties, deadlines, and commitments, weeds of negativity, frustration, and disappointment can take root. We may begin to focus on our shortcomings, failures, and fatigue rather than on the miracles God works through us.

Elizabeth Ann Seton, the founder of Catholic education in the United States, provides this beautiful advice to re-center our minds on God. Devotional reading helps us focus on God's agenda rather than our own. When we dedicate daily time to it, we can dig up the weeds that threaten our day-to-day mission to serve and nurture the beauty of God's presence within and around us.

Charleen Vinalon Doan
Bishop Dunne Catholic School
Dallas, Texas

SAINT FRANCIS DE SALES

You learn to speak by speaking, to study by studying, to run by running, to work by working, and just so, you learn to love by loving. All those who think to learn in any other way deceive themselves.

As teachers, we assign daily practice problems and review questions to help reinforce what students have learned. What is the equivalent in the spiritual life? We pray every day and teach our students to do the same.

When Jesus and saints like Francis de Sales speak about love, they are not referring solely to emotions. When we love or are loved by others, we feel good inside, but we shouldn't mistake the feelings for love itself. No, *love—caritas* or charity—is a virtue; it is a habit, a daily practice that becomes a part of us.

The practice of prayer leads us to experience love as we recognize, accept, and remember God's love for us. There are many prayer disciplines that help us do that: *lectio divina*, the profession of faith, the Angelus, the Liturgy of the Hours, the Rosary. They are *practices*. We do them again and again, regardless of how we feel, because they help us recall and celebrate God's infinite love for us.

The practice of prayer also leads us to share our experience of God's love with others. It isn't always easy to be generous with students who ignore us or are disrespectful. We often don't feel like loving them the way Christ loves them, but with prayerful practice we start to love them anyway. Grounded in God's *caritas*, we are able to share God's *caritas*.

Francis de Sales teaches us that we "learn to love by loving." As disciples, the best way we learn how to love is to remind ourselves—through the practice of prayer—how much God loves us. As educators, the best way we teach our students how to love is to teach them the daily practice of prayer. It's a habit that blossoms into virtue.

Jared Dees
TheReligionTeacher.com
South Bend, Indiana

Saint Francis of Assisi

Now for St. Francis nothing was ever in the background. We might say that his mind had no background, except perhaps that divine darkness out of which the divine love had called up every colored creature one by one. He saw everything as dramatic, distinct from its setting, not all of a piece like a picture but in action like a play. A bird went by him like an arrow; something with a story and a purpose, though it was a purpose of life and not a purpose of death. A bush could stop him like a brigand; and indeed he was as ready to welcome the brigand as the bush.

As teachers, we all know: Time is short and there are things to accomplish. Amid the flurry of classroom and after-school activities, our conversations with students can get caught up in the swirl and treated like another task to complete.

Answering a student's question or listening to a story about the dentist can seem like nothing more than an item on your to-do list—something to complete as efficiently and quickly as possible. Maybe we even feel tempted to multitask. *If I can just enter these grades while my student tells me about his favorite part of Harry Potter, then I can keep checking things off the list.*

However, Francis reminds us of the importance of simple attention. He recognized that every experience is saturated with the mystery and presence of the divine. As teachers, we know too that every encounter with our students is charged with the presence of God.

Our students come to us with stories and a purpose. Sometimes our greatest ministry can be to pay attention and recognize their beauty as children of God. As the poet Elizabeth Barrett Browning observed:

> Earth's crammed with heaven,
> And every common bush afire with God;
> But only he who sees, takes off his shoes.

Though we might keep our shoes on, we can turn our heads away from our computer screens, put down our grading pens, and behold the story unfolding in front of us.

Andrew Hoyt
Cristo Rey College Preparatory of Houston
Houston, Texas

Blessed Frederic Ozanam

Let us go to the poor!

Anti-Church sentiment was high in post-revolutionary France, and the University of Paris was no exception. In this hostile environment, one student, Frederic Ozanam, distinguished himself by speaking up in defense of the Catholic faith. A skeptical peer eventually confronted Frederic and asked, "You talk so much about the good of Catholicism, but tell me: What is your Church doing for the poor of our city?"

Recognizing that indeed Catholics were not doing enough, Frederic rallied his friends with the cry, "Let us go to the poor!" They did, and from that small group would grow the worldwide Society of St. Vincent de Paul.

While we rightly strive to make Catholic schools havens of faith, Frederic's story is a reminder that our role is not to shield students from challenges to their beliefs but to teach them to respond to such challenges constructively. Frederic's example illustrates three elements that can turn a potential roadblock into an opportunity for growth.

49

First, he stood strong in his faith, trusting the good he knew to be in the Church. Second, he was open to criticism, acknowledging that Catholics were falling short of Christ's call to service. Third, he took responsibility on himself. Rather than putting the blame elsewhere ("Let us go to the pastor! He should be promoting charity and justice!" "Let us go to the principal! This isn't my problem!"), Frederic first asked what his own part could be in improving the Church.

We have the same opportunity in our schools. A well-publicized statement by a bishop once prompted a fellow teacher of mine to assign a paper on immigration reform. When a parent complained that Catholic schools "had no right getting into political issues," the teacher listened and soon realized that no one had ever helped this parent to understand the foundations—or limits—of the Church's social teachings. The teacher remained committed to the immigration assignment, but she amended it to focus more on the issue's foundations in scripture and tradition, thus helping to fill a gap in knowledge about Catholic social teaching.

The courage to stand by one's beliefs, the humility to acknowledge our own and our institutions' shortcomings, and the initiative to look first for one's own role in addressing difficulties: these are the qualities that can help us—and help our students—thrive when confronted with challenges to the faith. Following the example of Frederic Ozanam, may our Catholic schools embody these principles as we instill them in all who pass through our classrooms.

Steve Calme
School of Theology and Ministry
Boston College Graduate Program
Boston, Massachusetts

VENERABLE ARCHBISHOP FULTON J. SHEEN

The Rosary is the book of the blind, where souls see and there enact the greatest drama of love the world has ever known; it is the book of the simple, which initiates them into mysteries and knowledge more satisfying than the education of other men; it is the book of the aged, whose eyes close upon the shadow of this world, and open on the substance of the next. The power of the Rosary is beyond description.

The theological truths and teachings of the Church are beautiful but can sometimes be inaccessible for children and adults alike. The power of the Rosary allows all the faithful to engage in Christ's deep and abiding love. It is particularly powerful when shared with children.

There is simply no greater spiritual boon than to engage children in our faith and tradition. As a teacher and catechist, I am consistently moved by the simultaneous simplicity and depth of their faith. I have especially loved teaching middle school students the beauty of the Rosary. As part of the lesson, each one makes his or her own knotted Rosary, and then we learn to pray it together. The enthusiasm and earnest desire each student conveys never fail to blow me away.

As an adult, I have a lot to learn from these children. When conflict arises, I often seek consolation in the teachings of the Church and forget the incredible gift of praying the Rosary—a time to "listen" to the lives of Jesus and Mary and allow them to speak to my life. It is often my heart that has to change, not my mind. In the Rosary, my heart encounters Jesus through Mary.

Christ's Incarnation, Death, and Resurrection are truly what Archbishop Fulton Sheen called the "greatest drama of love the world has ever known." The gift of the Rosary is that it allows us to access our story of salvation and journey with Christ. Like so many things in the life of faith, my students and their natural enthusiasm for engaging in this kind of prayer have taught me that "the power of the Rosary is beyond description."

Aaron Wall
St. Pius X Parish
Granger, Indiana

Saint Ignatius of Loyola

*It is an ordinary experience that, where there is
much contradiction, much fruit will follow. . . .*

Confined to his bed as he convalesced from a serious
leg injury, Ignatius of Loyola had little to occupy
his time except for reading and daydreaming. He wanted to read stories about gallant knights and chivalry,
but he found only two books—one on the life of Christ
and one on the lives of the saints. As he read these
books, he began daydreaming about imitating the saints
and giving up everything to follow Christ.

At other times, Ignatius would daydream of being
a courtier who performed brave deeds and won the
love of a noble lady. Ignatius soon began to notice a
difference in the aftereffects of these imaginings. When
he thought about life at court and its many physical
pleasures, he felt delighted and happy, but soon after
he stopped his dreaming, he would feel dry and dis-
satisfied. On the other hand, when he thought about
giving up his possessions and living a life of poverty
following Christ, he not only felt consoled during the
daydream but remained satisfied and joyful long after
he put these thoughts aside.

We all need time to reflect. In our busy lives, we
have many moving experiences and then immediately

turn to the next thing without stopping to ponder how we are doing in the midst of it all. In many cases, our students are no different, switching from class to class, assignment to assignment, and activity to activity without the time or space to think about their lives, their learning, and all the emotions connected to their experiences.

Ignatius had his own distractions as a soldier and courtier until he found himself homebound with plenty of time not only to read what he never would have read otherwise but also to ponder the feelings and desires these stories awoke in him. His experiences of reading and daydreaming, and his reflections on his mental and emotional responses, led to his conversion and to his development of guidelines for discernment that have taught countless teachers and people of faith a simple process: experience, reflection, and action. What a simple and profound gift that all of us can use!

Teachers and students alike need experiences that make us feel and think deeply. Then, we need time to reflect on and learn from those experiences so they might produce an abundant crop of spiritual fruit. Finally, we need to act on Christ's constant invitation to become ever more like him in our daily lives.

How can you set aside time each day for prayerful reflection to see how God is working in you and who God is calling you to be? How can you give your students the same gift, structuring opportunities for them to experience, reflect, and act?

Thomas Bambrick, S.J.
Jesuit First Studies Program
Fordham University
Bronx, New York

Saint Ignatius of Loyola

Whole Surrender

Receive, O Lord, all my liberty. Take my memory, my understanding, and my entire will. Whatsoever I have or hold, you have given me; I give it all back to you and surrender it wholly to be governed by your will. Give me only your love and your grace, and I am rich enough and ask for nothing more.

Ignatius, how did you reach such a state of freedom? So much inside of me begs for more control over this student here, that lesson there. I feel hard-wired to accumulate that which you prayed to release: memories, understanding, and choices. What will I be left with if I give it all away? How will the passersby recognize my uniqueness? Can I trust God to safeguard everything I own?

Ignatius, is this spiritual exercise intentionally trying? Did it help free you from the biological bindings of your body and mind? I see hope in your words as I begin to shed all the purposeful parts of me that have been evolutionarily programmed to survive. Layers removed, my empty human vessel exposed, all that I wanted to keep now given away. Left with nothing worldly and filled with pure substance, my body begins to pulse with love and grace alone.

Ignatius, how did I ever want more? My improbable existence, born from the divinely inspired meeting of my greatest grandparents, should have already burst my heart with gratitude. How was my focus just my classroom, my own office, my daily human demands in the face of such mystery? Granted, I must be gentle with myself when the next need arises, as the beauty of that primal program makes me human. But your exercise takes me beyond to the gift of this next breath, belonging not to me.

Gregory Gomez
Cristo Rey Preparatory of Houston
Houston, Texas

SAINT IGNATIUS OF LOYOLA

AD MAJOREM DEI GLORIAM

For the greater glory of God.

Students ask many questions. Some can be simple, such as "Why do we have to do homework?" Others may be more serious like, "What am I going to do when I grow up?"

I can remember asking a simple question as a freshman in high school, and the answer changed my life. All our teachers at the Jesuit high school told us that we were required to write the letters "AMDG" at the top of every paper and test. Failure to do so would result in a five-point deduction from our grade. Many students complained, but the faculty was consistent in this request, and everyone did it. One day in class, I asked our religion teacher what AMDG meant.

Our teacher told us that it was Latin and stood for *ad majorem Dei gloriam,* which means "for the greater glory of God." He went on to tell us that this brief phrase was chosen as the motto for the Jesuits—the foundation of the spirituality they live by. Then he taught us a simple prayer, the Examen, which would help us keep the awareness of God in our minds. He suggested that we take a few minutes at the end of each day to review what had occurred. Look at our blessings and give thanks. And then ask, "Where was God during this day?"

As a freshman in high school, I learned how a simple phrase and prayer can shape and direct everything we do. To be inspired by Ignatius's AMDG means that any action or work can be spiritually meritorious if performed to give glory and honor to God. To pray the Examen at the end of the day helps us see how God is at work in our lives.

These lessons have been instrumental in my life as a priest, teacher, mentor, and spiritual director. May each of us seek to live for God's glory and to find God in all things.

Fr. Joe Carey, C.S.C.
Alliance for Catholic Education
University of Notre Dame
Notre Dame, Indiana

Saint Irenaeus of Lyons

*For the glory of God is a living man; and the
life of man consists in beholding God.*

How profound is this insight of Irenaeus of Lyons, a second-century bishop, who argued vigorously against Gnosticism and its denial of the perplexing and joyful mystery of the Incarnation and the radical hope it brings to humanity. This bold claim, sometimes translated "the glory of God is a man fully alive," captures so beautifully the fundamental dignity of the human person, made in the image and likeness of God.

As educators, can we imagine a more inspiring vision for our work, called as we are to help young people become "fully alive" as they grow in faith and develop their God-given talents? In an age when educational discourse is focused on how our students are "falling behind" internationally, and when a student's value is often determined by his or her ability to achieve prosperity, Irenaeus insists that in the formation of our students, far more is at stake.

Of course, some days it can take the vision and charity of a saint to see our students as the "glory of God"! They may resist our carefully planned lessons. They may ignore our efforts to help them learn and improve. We may stumble by snapping, procrastinating, or complaining. However, these are precisely the times when Irenaeus's words can remind us of the eternal relevance of the vocation of teaching and challenge us to shoulder its inevitable crosses in a spirit of hope and love, knowing that we are blessed with the privilege to promote the abiding dignity of the human person and build the city of God.

John Staud
Alliance for Catholic Education
University of Notre Dame
Notre Dame, Indiana

SAINT ISAAC JOGUES

GRACE TO OVERCOME

Called the "Apostle of the Mohawks" and known to the Mohawks themselves as Ondessonk, "the indomitable one," Isaac Jogues dedicated his life to sharing the Gospel with seventeenth-century Native American Indians. One year, Isaac and a group of others were captured by Mohawk warriors.

He was held captive for months, enduring multiple tortures. He spent much time in prayer near a great tree in which he carved a cross. Half clad in shaggy furs, he would kneel in the snow among the icicled rocks, bowing in adoration before the emblem of his faith—his only hope.

Eventually, Isaac was freed by the Dutch. Though safe, he set forth to minister to the Mohawks in the same place he was tortured! His bravery and lack of ill will impressed all the Mohawks, but when disease and famine broke out, the Bear clan faction put him to death.

Mr. Bodart never helps me. And he can't coach!" It was late November, the beginning of basketball season, and my athletic director had called a meeting with this student and me in order to address some behavioral issues. Flabbergasted at my student's accusation, I felt a surge of anger as my mind raced through all the times I had tutored him at lunch and provided individual instruction after practice. For two years I helped him, and this is how he was thanking me?

If there is anyone who understands the sometimes thanklessness of teaching, it is Isaac Jogues. He left his homeland, risking his life to share the love of Christ to strangers. Instead of being thanked, he was captured, tortured multiple times, and eventually killed. He had every right to be angry and to abandon his mission, but through prayer, Isaac received the grace and humility necessary to forgive his captors and continue his work.

As teachers, it is often easy to harbor ill will toward our students when they don't appreciate our hard work and long hours. The temptation is to yell, "Look at all I've done for you!" Stories like that of Isaac Jogues remind us that we are not elite missionaries who have come to educate the lesser. We are servants of Christ, needing as much grace and humility as those we serve. It is through prayer, as Isaac showed us, that we receive the grace and humility necessary to surrender our righteous anger, forgive our students, and continue our work of sharing Christ's love.

It took several Isaac Jogues–like moments of prayer, bowing before the Lord and asking for the grace and humility to forgive, before I was ready to surrender my anger and resume helping this student. To my surprise and the student's credit, he came to me one day and said, "Thanks, Coach." With grace and humility we—teachers and students alike—can become missionaries for Christ.

Tom Bodart
Moreau Seminary Postulant Program
Notre Dame, Indiana

Saint John Baptist de La Salle

AMBASSADORS FOR CHRIST

*Because you are ambassadors and ministers of
Jesus Christ in the work that you do, you must
act as representing Jesus Christ.*

John Baptist de La Salle is the patron saint of teachers. This French priest gave up personal wealth in order to dedicate his life to teaching the poor. Like St. Paul before him (2 Cor 5:20), John Baptist referred to Christians as *ambassadors*, accredited diplomats who are sent to represent a particular country in its relationship with another country. This role commands respect and admiration.

If you're in Catholic education, you know you're a minister, but did you know that you are also an ambassador? You are an ambassador of Christ to your students and their families, "accredited" by your baptism and "sent" via your calling to teach in a Catholic school. Your duty is to touch the hearts of your students, representing Christ by the spirit of God. Just as leaders of countries rely on ambassadors for daily contact with other leaders, so your students often rely on you for experiencing the love, truth, and mercy of Christ.

May we never take this awe-inspiring call lightly. With the title ambassador comes great responsibility to know Christ in our own lives so that we might represent him well to our students and their families. We are accredited. We are sent. Let us represent him well!

Fr. Brian O'Brien
Bishop Kelley High School
Tulsa, Oklahoma

Saint John Bosco

There is a great wisdom in those words of the Holy Spirit: "Be angry but sin not." I would like to add something further. If, as teachers and educators, all the hard work and stress and strain we have to put up with seem to be getting nowhere in our work with young people, then perhaps we should take a good look at ourselves.

Anger. It is a feeling that can be all too common in the life of an educator. Whether it is the daydreaming adolescent that we just can't get to focus, incessant petitions to repeat what we just said, or the constant struggle to get a class to behave properly at an assembly, it can easily feel as though the world is against us. The question is, What are we to do when we begin to lose hope in the midst of anger?

It is okay to be angry, John Bosco said, but we must be cautious about how we handle it. To respond to students in anger only teaches them to do the same. No matter how difficult they may be, our vocation calls us to respond as Jesus did—through constant love and charity.

It is not always easy to live up to the standard set by our quintessential role model. When anger seems to be getting the better of us, "we should take a good look at ourselves," stepping back to allow room for prayer and reflection before acting on our emotions. By mentally and spiritually preparing ourselves to handle frustration and anger, we show our students how to overcome their own. And to the degree that we model patient instruction and self-discipline, our students will come to know the patient love of Christ.

Greg O'Donnell
St. John the Evangelist Catholic School
Pensacola, Florida

Saint John Bosco

A Just Cause

When one is convinced that his cause is just,
he will fear nothing.

In my first year as a teacher, when I arrived at school each morning, I would sit in the parking lot feeling very afraid. I would be afraid that today everything would fall apart. I would imagine my classroom looking like the pictures in *Miss Nelson Is Missing!*—spitballs flying, desks overturned, paper airplanes pegging a student's temple, and loud talking despite my desperate attempts to restore order. Each morning, I would sit in my car until the to-do list in my head got too long, and then I would drag my heavy heart into school. I was convinced that my imperfections would lead me to failure.

One particular morning, fear had just begun to take hold when a deep sense of peace washed over me. I realized, in the words of John Bosco, "Education is a just cause!" I have everything I need to be successful. I have what it takes to change a life, inspire, or just pick up the pieces and try again. Why else would God have called me to this profession, this just cause?

I considered the often-mentioned teaching mantra about the significance of "crafting relationships" with the students. The word *relationship* has broad connotations that range from life-giving connectedness to cursory interaction. For those who strive to be great educators, we are definitely called to the former—to craft the types of relationships with students that result in becoming their coach, their mentor, their Confirmation sponsor, or even a speaker at their wedding. A just cause indeed!

During that first year of teaching, I was still afraid that the students would learn nothing, but over time teaching has become a path of internal growth where I learn that each of us possesses the power to accomplish far greater things than our fears aspire to hinder.

Elizabeth Brands
Saint Catherine School
Tulsa, Oklahoma

Saint John Bosco

It is easier to . . . threaten a boy than to persuade him. Yes, indeed, it is more fitting to be persistent in punishing our own impatience and pride than to correct the boys! We must be firm but kind, and be patient with them.

*P*ersuade him? Since when should a teacher or a dean at a school spend time persuading the students? Schools are supposed to be firm bastions of discipline and values! Has school discipline eroded such that adults are reduced to trying to persuade children to discipline? How could John Bosco advocate such action?

As John Bosco undoubtedly knew, offending students must be punished according to a just and logical process—but the great gift of a superior education is that an adult takes the time necessary to persuade students of the soundness of that process. This means explaining the necessity of rules in a school, reinforcing the fairness of the punishment, and patiently reminding students that their punishment is only a means to correct behavior, not a judgment on their person. Those words are the essence of discipline that cooperates with—and enhances—the larger educational project.

As dean of a Catholic high school in Austin, Texas, I spent hours attempting to persuade students of the rightness of punishments that had already been justly determined. Those hours often seemed fruitless. However, the last sentence of John Bosco's quotation reminds us that discipline combines the firmness of a just system with the compassion of talking it out in a way a child can understand.

Often children just want to be heard, and some students who arrived at my office with bluster and anger left accepting their detention after I offered an ear to their grievance. In this way, great educators teach the same discipline that God the Father practices: a judge's firmness in punishing wickedness with a parent's mercy in administering love.

Dan Reynolds
Peabody College of Education Graduate Program
Vanderbilt University
Nashville, Tennessee

Blessed John Henry Newman

*God has created me to do him some definite
service. He has committed some work to me
which he has not committed to another. I have
my mission. I may never know it in this life,
but I shall be told it in the next. I am a link in
a chain, a bond of connection between persons.
He has not created me for naught. I shall do
good; I shall do his work.*

When I was in high school, my friends and I spent
far too much time memorizing *Saturday Night
Live* skits and incorporating the dialogue into our every-
day conversations. Among my favorites was a series of
skits by satirist (now United States senator) Al Franken
titled "Daily Affirmation with Stuart Smalley." Franken
parodied a self-help guru who would shower his guests
with advice such as "You need a checkup from the neck
up!" and "That's just stinkin' thinkin'!" My favorite by
far was, "You're good enough, you're smart enough, and
doggone it—people like you!"

Even though I still laugh every time I see "Daily
Affirmation," I have come to understand that the skit
actually points to at least one fundamental flaw in the
way that far too many of us see ourselves. As John
Henry Newman's famous meditation reveals, the life of
discipleship—and indeed the life of an educator—does

not require us to experience ourselves as "enough" of anything. Instead, it is a personal invitation from God to accept our indispensable role in proclaiming the gospel.

There are neither fixed nor relative standards for what constitutes "good enough," "smart enough," or anything else "enough" in the Christian journey. Jesus calls us not so that we may have "enough" but instead so that we may have life and have it to the full. And we cannot truly accept the invitation to discipleship until we recognize that each one of us plays a unique and integral role in helping the rest of the world hear and respond to the Good News. "For me to be a saint," said Thomas Merton, "means to be myself." It is at once both confounding and thrilling that our sanctification ultimately rests on nothing more than our own willingness to discover who we really are—and to help our students do the same.

John Schoenig
Alliance for Catholic Education
University of Notre Dame
Notre Dame, Indiana

Saint John of the Cross

Silence

Whenever anything disagreeable or displeasing happens to you, remember Christ crucified and be silent.

In 2011, Felipe Passos pledged to raise enough money so that he and members of his prayer group could attend World Youth Day in 2013. Six months before the event, two thieves broke into his house to steal the hard-earned cash. Felipe refused to give the money to them. The thieves shot him and left him to die.

Through the grace of God and the prayers of his family, the twenty-three-year-old miraculously survived. When World Youth Day 2013 arrived, Felipe Passos not only attended but was invited to speak. Now wheelchair-bound, Felipe said, "This is my cross, the cross the Lord sent me to come closer to him, to live more openly his grace and love." When the three million young people began to clap, he cut them off. "Silence! Let's listen to the Holy Spirit!" Then he asked, "What is the cross that the Lord has given you? What is the cross that he wants you to carry for his love?"

Teaching can be our way of the cross. We begin the year full of energy to work in our corner of the Lord's vineyard, but before long we become burdened by the needs of our students, busyness, and noise. It is then that we most need silence—time to be still and know that he is God (Ps 46:10). In silence, we can hear the Holy Spirit's reminder that it is not about what we do but about what God does through us. In silence, the Spirit can help us discover anew that we do not carry the cross of our daily work alone. Christ becomes our Simon, helping us carry the cross for his love.

So in the midst of the whirlwind of our days, "remember Christ crucified" and then, "Silence! Let's listen to the Holy Spirit!"

Carl Loesch
Marian High School
Mishawaka, Indiana

Saint John Paul II

Be Not Afraid

*Faced with today's problems and disappoint-
ments, many people will try to escape from
their responsibility. Escape in selfishness . . .
escape in drugs, escape in violence, escape in
indifference and cynical attitudes. I propose to
you the option of love, which is the opposite
of escape.*

As a teacher, you may wear many different hats, but ultimately, you have one job: to love. Though it sounds simple, in a society where the culture of death is a constant reality, this job proves to be an interminable task. Loving students does not just mean letting them know you care about them. It means continually orienting them toward truth so that they don't lose themselves in the world's deceptions. It means setting their hearts on fire for what is good and beautiful so that they won't embrace indifference. It means guiding them in the way of virtue so that they don't sink into cynicism.

Each day, as John Paul II said, both students and teachers are faced with seemingly insurmountable problems and disappointments. To teach a student who cannot write a complete sentence to tackle a college essay may seem impossible. To see a student who has spent countless hours in tutoring fail yet again can bring feelings of despair. To watch a student who has worked tirelessly to learn kindness lash out in frustration may lead to a sense of defeat.

John Paul II proposes that, in the face of these obstacles, we cannot escape by becoming discouraged, selfish, or closed off; instead, we must love. We must make ourselves vulnerable—even when it means becoming susceptible to disappointment again. Only then do we open ourselves to Christ's promised victory. As John Paul II exhorted often in the fearless words of Christ, we must "Be not afraid!"

Mary Forr
Saint Peter's School
Washington, DC

Saint John the Baptist

*I baptize you with water; but he who is mighti-
er than I is coming, the thong of whose sandals
I am not worthy to untie; he will baptize you
with the Holy Spirit and with fire. . . .*

Luke 3:16–17

From the time John leapt in Elizabeth's womb at Mary's presence, he was focused on his call to prepare the way for Jesus. And as we know from the Gospels, John lived out his vocation passionately by offering baptism to all he encountered. As evident in Luke's gospel, the crowds were hungry to know how to ready themselves for the Messiah. John offered unin-hibited, raw honesty to the people seeking baptism, challenging them to become the best versions of them-selves as they prepared for the coming of Jesus.

At Trinity Catholic High School in Newton, Massa-chusetts, the students frequently led the school's week-ly Liturgy of the Word service. I was often humbled by the raw and honest personal stories they offered in their gospel reflections. They were amazing at depict-ing the presence of Jesus in both hardship and tri-umph, and they were unafraid, like John the Baptist, to close their reflections with a call to action: "Seek understanding before judgment!" or "Open your eyes to those in need around you!"

Who are the John the Baptists in your life who call you to action?

"In the name of the Father, and of the Son and of the Holy Spirit." These are the words we use when we enter a church and bless ourselves with holy water from the baptismal font. As we do this, let us center our hearts, asking the Lord to grant us the fresh start of baptism when we next enter our classrooms. Additionally, let us ask ourselves how John the Baptist would challenge us to improve this week so that we may be prepared for the presence of Jesus.

Kelly Surapaneni
Trinity Catholic High School
Newton, Massachusetts

SAINT JOHN VIANNEY

ON COLLECTIVE PRAYER

*Private prayer is like straw scattered here and
there: If you set it on fire it makes a lot of little
flames. But gather these straws into a bundle
and light them, and you get a mighty fire, rising like a column into the sky; public prayer
is like that.*

When I think about the most powerful experiences
I have had in my school, I think about collective
moments of prayer. I picture the students sitting next
to their grandparents at Mass on the feast day of Our
Lady of Guadalupe. I imagine first graders belting out
"Halleluiah! He is Born!" at our Christmas concert. I
recall eighth graders offering intentions for each other
in the classroom. I see the staff kneeling in adoration in
front of the Eucharist. Each of these moments reminds
me of John Vianney's powerful image of public, collective prayer as "a mighty fire."

Community is powerful. A community that recog-
nizes that its bonds have been created by God is even
more so. Community offers us a chance not only to
pray together but also to be our best selves among each
other. Our actions and conversations become forms
of prayer. They proclaim our belief that God lives in
each one of us. Whenever I am tempted to turn inward,

to keep my relationship with God private as if only God and I are in on the conversation, I gently remind myself to turn outward and join my intentions with those of the rest of my faith community.

We are meant to live in relationship with others. The Holy Trinity models this for us, showing that God's essential nature is relational. As a priest I know often says, "If God is in relationship, who am I to think I can do it on my own?" Or, in the imagery of John Vianney, why settle for little flames, when we might enkindle a roaring fire? When we embrace this truth, when we embrace each other, we truly honor God, our communal prayer "rising like a column into the sky."

Katie Olson
Our Lady of Charity Catholic School
Cicero, Illinois

Saint Joseph, Father of Jesus

*And Joseph too went up from Galilee from the
town of Nazareth to Judea, to the city of David
that is called Bethlehem, because he was of
the house and family of David, to be enrolled
with Mary, his betrothed, who was with child.*

Luke 2:4–5

In our family's Nativity scene, Joseph holds a lantern
aloft and gazes down on his infant son and wife, lead-
ing viewers to do the same. In effect, Joseph is making
sure the light is always focused on Jesus while he himself slips into the background. He does this so easily,
in fact, that we can overlook how essential he was to
Jesus' life and ministry.

Joseph married Mary against popular convention of
the time; he fearlessly took his family to Egypt ahead
of Herod's agents; and he labored as a carpenter to provide a stable home for Jesus. As we look more closely,
we begin to realize just how wonderful a role model
Joseph is for all those who work in the background to
help Catholic schools flourish.

Our family has just moved back to Beth's home-
town, and we are blessed to send our children to the
same parish school she and her brothers attended.
While some things at the school are new, many things

remain the same: the commitment to deep faith and excellent education, the diversity of family backgrounds, and the many parishioners who have volunteered for years in the school and parish. During the recent service for our daughter's first Reconciliation, the cantor was the same woman who was cantor when Beth was in school. She has also been the cafeteria supervisor for more than twenty-five years! She is like the Joseph of our Nativity scene come to life.

Legions of talented people work behind the scenes to help Catholic schools continue their ministries. They welcome visitors, move cafeteria lines along, and tutor students; they make phone calls, maintain websites, and serve as cantors. Like Joseph, they "hold aloft a lantern," allowing principals, teachers, and parents to keep their students' focus on Jesus as they learn to love and serve God and the world.

Max and Beth Engel
St. Pius X/St. Leo School
Omaha, Nebraska

Saint Joseph of Cupertino

The Flying Saint

*In class, Joseph of Cupertino never could read
very well. He was quick to anger with other
students. Sickly as a child, his father died when
he was young and he was raised by his mother.
He'd often lose his train of thought and couldn't
finish the story he was telling. St. Joseph was
so prone to distraction that he would drop all
his books when the church bell rang, and his
classmates mocked him all the more. Frequently staring into space and daydreaming earned
him the nickname "Bocca Aperta," Italian for
"Open Mouth."*

This childhood portrait of Joseph of Cupertino will
cause many teachers to think of students they
know with similar academic and behavioral challenges. We all encounter students who struggle socially,
face difficult home environments, have special learning needs, or lack motivation and focus. Despite these
students' best efforts, they often exist at the margins.

When we look upon these students, do we do so
with patience, compassion, and with confidence, certain that God-given gifts are indeed present but perhaps
unnoticed or unrealized?

Young Joseph of Cupertino reminds us that we should not overlook the grace at work in such students' lives. Indeed, Joseph grew up to be known as "the flying saint"—for when deep in prayer and reflection, he was known to levitate! In his humility, he achieved a closeness and connection with God and Our Lady that was so transformative he reached heights that no other human could. His example speaks forcefully to the inherent dignity and boundless potential of all students. Despite their outward awkwardness, disability, and brokenness, their souls can still soar, their hearts can fully elevate to God.

Jim Frabutt
ACE Teaching Exceptional Children
University of Notre Dame
Notre Dame, Indiana

Saint Juan Diego Cuauhtlatoatzin

In December 1531, Juan Diego was making his regular, fifteen-mile trek to morning Mass when the Blessed Mother appeared to him on Tepeyac Hill, the outskirts of what is now Mexico City. She asked him to go to the bishop and request that a shrine be built at Tepeyac, where she promised to pour out her grace on all who would worship there. Juan Diego obeyed, but as he was a poor farmer with no social standing, the bishop did not believe him and sent him away, demanding proof that his message was true.

Juan Diego returned to Tepeyac to find Mary waiting for him. She told him to climb the hill and pick the roses that were—although it was winter—in bloom. At Mary's direction, Juan Diego wrapped them in his cloak and returned to the bishop with his proof. When he revealed the flowers, a beautiful image of Mary appeared on the fabric of his coat. The bishop ordered the church be built, and within six years, six million people had converted to

> *Catholicism. Juan Diego lived the rest of his life*
> *as a hermit in a hut near the church.*

Juan Diego humbly accepted the Lord's challenge through Mary, Our Lady of Guadalupe, to spread the gospel by—literally—building a church. Think of the faith, tenacity, and trust it took for him to do this: to believe Mary's appearance was real, to summon the courage to take her message to a bishop (and endure his rejection), and finally to trust that Mary would revisit him at Tepeyac to provide the proof the bishop demanded. Clearly, Juan Diego knew God was calling him to service, and he was relentless in his pursuit of that goal. What a role model he offers us.

As Catholic school teachers or administrators, we have accepted the Lord's challenge to spread the gospel by forming our students into the strong, smart, faith-filled leaders of tomorrow. This is our call to service, and to keep our eyes on that goal requires the faith, trust, and tenacity of Juan Diego.

We are not poor farmers with no social standing, but we know the poverty of spirit that comes after an emotionally exhausting day. We may not have to endure a bishop's rejection, but we know rejection when our lessons fall on deaf ears or, worse, prompt a phone call from a disapproving parent. We may not receive a personal visit from Mary or walk fifteen miles to Mass (multiple times a week, no less), but we persevere in our devotion to God and in our daily response to God's call to teach and care for our students.

With Juan Diego as our guide, may we aim today for the higher goals to which we have been called.

Gena Robinson
Louverture Cleary School
Port-au-Prince, Haiti

Saint Julie Billiart

Speak with respect to your children if you want them to respect you and love you . . . otherwise, no good can be done.

When I first began teaching high school theology in Mississippi, the most surprising moments occurred when students "didn't get" something that seemed utterly clear to me. I soon learned that I carried biases from my East Coast upbringing and education into the classroom—biases from which I unwittingly taught, giving my students absolutely no context for understanding certain topics.

One spring, the juniors read one of my favorite articles on Catholic social teaching. The author wrote critically of how we have lost sight of the need for kinship and community as families have become increasingly insular.

After I excitedly spoke about the complexity of the author's argument, all twenty-one juniors looked confused. "Wait. What do you mean there are places where people don't know their neighbors? Do you not know your neighbors at home, Miss Lazor?" asked one female student.

The quarterback of the football team added, "I can name everyone that lives on my street. My mama has me mow the older people's lawns, especially if they're veterans."

My students couldn't relate to the reading because they couldn't imagine life without community at its center. Their lived experience was the perfect antidote to the frustrated author's words regarding "American" culture. My students were American, but this wasn't their culture. What a lesson for me.

Over time, my most cherished moments with my students unfolded when I was able to express my great respect for the richness of Mississippi's people and culture. As I came to love my students' home, I came to realize that I was blessed to be walking on holy ground, and this is when my true teaching began.

Julie Billiart founded the Sisters of Notre Dame de Namur with the mission that all people are in need of formation. She knew, however, that this formation only began after respect was established between the ones teaching and the ones learning. As she speaks of the importance of respecting our students, I can't help but think that she was aware that sometimes students are the best teachers.

Emily Lazor
St. Joseph Catholic School
Madison, Mississippi

Saint Katharine Drexel

*Peacefully do at each moment what at the
moment needs to be done.*

As teachers, our to-do lists are usually much longer
than we could ever accomplish. We feel stretched
between responsibilities to our students, their parents,
administrators, and our own family and friends. We
multitask throughout the day, managing classroom
behavior while assisting one student with a problem
or recording attendance while collecting homework
and listening to morning announcements. The frenetic
pace of a typical school day often leaves me feeling
exhausted but efficient. I enjoy looking back at my day
and ticking off the many tasks I accomplished, despite
the many more that are still left on my to-do list.

But what is the cost of being so concerned with
what needs to be done? How often do we find it difficult to be fully present to the task or person at hand
because we are too busy worrying about everything
else we need to do and everywhere else we need to
be? I know I have spent more after-school tutoring ses-
sions than I'd like to admit only halfway present while
explaining math and science concepts. The other half
of my attention and energy is spent silently scanning
through the remaining items on my to-do list, trying

to figure out how to accomplish everything before the day's end.

Katharine Drexel reassures us that whatever task is before us—grading papers, sitting in a faculty meeting, comforting a child, or supervising at recess—is what deserves our time, attention, and gifts in that moment. This frees us to give our whole selves to whatever aspect of the ministry of teaching is before us and to be at peace knowing that we are doing God's work.

Sarah Lamphier
Holy Cross College
Notre Dame, Indiana

SAINT LAURA MONTOYA

MEETING THEM WHERE THEY ARE

*Necesitaba mujeres intrépidas, valientes, infla-
madas en el amor de Dios, que pudieran asimi-
lar su vida a la de los pobres habitantes de la
selva, para levantarlos hacia Dios.*

*("I needed intrepid women, brave, swollen
in the love of God. They could assimilate his
life to the poor inhabitants of the jungle, to lift
them up to God.")*

These words by recently canonized Laura Montoya
summarize the vocation of teaching and challenge
us all, men as well as women, to unite our lives with
the children we teach.

Laura originally became a teacher to support her
family, which had become destitute when her father
was killed in the Colombian Civil War. She taught in her
home state of Antioquia for more than twenty years. At
the age of forty, moved by the prejudice she had seen
directed toward the native population of her country,
Laura left Antioquia to live with the indigenous peo-
ples in the jungle of Colombia. There she learned that
teaching was so much more than transmitting knowledge and cultivating skills; it was meeting the children
where they were, presenting the gospel in a way they
could understand.

Through such assimilation, Madre Laura sought to develop children as persons destined for eternal life with God. Madre Laura and her followers were ridiculed and despised for their work, even by Church authorities. But Madre Laura challenged her followers—and everyone who teaches—to adopt a "pedagogy of love" in the classroom. Based on the gospel, this pedagogy demands that we teach by looking at the world through the eyes of our students, not our own.

This pedagogy also asks us to reach out to children "on the periphery," those who are poor, rejected, and isolated. Madre Laura asks for "intrepid" followers because her pedagogy of love demands that we confront the structural sins that mire children in poverty and neglect. Those of us who teach in the United States must address the scandal of child poverty in the midst of staggering wealth. Let us pray that, like Madre Laura, our hearts will be enflamed by God's grace to agitate as we advocate for the children we love.

Clark Power
Play Like a Champion Today
University of Notre Dame
Notre Dame, Indiana

SAINT LAWRENCE

Turn me over; I'm done on this side.

Long before Larry the Cable Guy got laughs on the Blue Collar Comedy Tour, the Church honored Lawrence, who tradition tells us while burning at the stake quipped, "Turn me over; I'm done on this side." I've recalled that story many times, initially because I found it so funny (what did those within earshot think?), and now because I marvel at Lawrence's faith that produced the words, the legend, or both.

Humor is integral to an enduring spiritual journey. Often we can focus on the dour, doom-and-gloom side of faith until we consider Christ's message to "be like children to enter the kingdom." According to *Psychology Today*, the average four-year-old laughs three hundred times a day (compared to the average forty-year-old, who laughs only four). Pure and simple, or cutting and dark, humor helps us handle what life throws our way.

The '80s rock band Depeche Mode had it wrong when they sang, "God has a sick sense of humor." Perhaps you have seen the picture of Jesus with his head thrown back, mouth open in laughter. I imagine him smiling wryly at some of our goings-on, his bright eyes shining even through tears. We can glimpse this sensibility in the smiles of Pope Francis, who cautioned in a recent apostolic exhortation, "There are Christians whose lives seem like Lent without Easter."

I have heard that first responders who last the longest on the job use humor in their harrowing work. Their laughter may follow a good cry, but it's healing all the same. Those of us who evangelize in our vocation as educators are something like first responders. We may do well to use some compassionate humor at times in entertaining our students' doubts and crises. The Church, in her wisdom, is right to celebrate these saints who illuminate our shadows.

Sorin Spohn
Saint Xavier High School
Louisville, Kentucky

Saint Luke

Seeing Faith with Fresh Eyes

*Then astonishment seized them all and they
glorified God and, struck with awe, they said,
"We have seen incredible things today!"*

Luke 5:26

My daughter Meaghan plays on a local community basketball team. She and her teammates are nine years old. They all go to different schools; their families are diverse by nearly every measure. As nine-year-olds often do, Meaghan recently asked one of her teammates Kayla to our house for a Saturday night sleepover. Since we would be going to Mass in the morning, I got her dad's permission for her to join us.

Sunday morning arrived, and after some pancakes and prodding, we headed to eleven o'clock. Mass. As Kayla entered our church, she immediately started taking in every detail of every object she saw. It was clear she had never been in a Catholic church. The questions began: "Who is that?" "Why are there flowers in front of her?" "Why are there nine candles over the door?" "What is that water for?" "Why do you move your hands like that?" On it went. Nothing was taken for granted by this bright, inquisitive girl.

I answered her questions as best as I could. I was awed by her spirit to learn and moved to see familiar images and symbols through new, wondering eyes. The answers to Kayla's questions reminded me that we are loved, that we do not walk alone, that we are part of a centuries-long chain of (often flawed) people doing their best to love Jesus. How often have I missed that? Worse, how often have I taken it for granted?

The students in front of us can help us see our "old" world as fresh and alive with God's presence and providence. Next time you enter your classroom or church, think of what Kayla might be asking you as she looks at the treasures you've seen a million times before. The answers will have you praising God and saying, "I have seen amazing things today!"

Judy Madden
Christ the King Parish
South Bend, Indiana

Saint Marcellin Champagnat

Becoming Nothing for God

God does great things with nothing.

Marcellin Champagnat, the patron saint of teachers and founder of the Marist Brothers, was dedicated to serving the poor through education. He wrote the words above in a letter to one of his brothers in 1823. One might think that he was referring to the students. Considering their humble beginnings, it would be rather grand to imagine them rising above that "nothing" status and doing great things as a result of their stellar education. Surprisingly though, Marcellin is referring to one of the new novices he is expecting to join the Marists. He introduces this man in the letter simply as "a nobody."

If I heard someone—especially a mentor or superior—referring to me as "a nobody," I'd be a little offended. Where is the encouragement? Where is the respect? Where is the love?

We all desire to be somebody in this world. Maybe we have a list of impressive accomplishments we can cite. Maybe we want to be recognized for our hard work. Maybe we wish to make a difference in people's lives. However it happens, it feels good to be somebody.

But Marcellin Champagnat invites us to a deeper insight: maybe it's actually better to be "a nobody." Think about it. If we begin as nobody but simple children of God, then there is nothing—no pride or vanity or selfishness—to get in the way. God will be able to use us however God pleases to accomplish whatever God desires.

Although we sometimes feel a deep need to be recognized or to exalt ourselves, let us work and pray for the humility that Marcellin Champagnat counsels. In making ourselves less, we can allow God to work through us to better serve our students. God will use our nothingness for God's glory.

Stacey Brandt
Notre Dame-Cathedral Latin School
Cleveland, Ohio

SAINT MARCELLIN CHAMPAGNAT

*Tell your children that Jesus and Mary love
them all very much: those who are good
because they resemble Jesus Christ, who is
infinitely good; those who are not yet good,
because they will become so. Tell them that
the Blessed Virgin also loves them, because she
is the mother of all the children in our schools.*

During every moment of the day, educators have
the opportunity to communicate God's love.
Whether a cheerful teacher is easing anxieties on the
first day of class, an encouraging coach is teaching a
new skill, or a principal is sternly but lovingly guiding a
group of students to become their best selves, educators
have the incredible opportunity—and responsibility—
to bring students into a tangible experience of God's
consoling mercy and ever-present love.

Marcellin Champagnat suggests an all-too-often
overlooked manner of teaching God's love: put it in
simple and direct words. By telling your students about
God's love for them, you will help them make sense
of the gifts in their lives, and you will offer meaning-
ful consolation for the inevitable moments when they
will experience the world's—or their own—brokenness.

The best teachers find a variety of ways to present
information. After all, each student learns differently,

and no one way of teaching reading or algebra or a foreign language will succeed with all learners. In the essential work of drawing students into the experience of being loved, do not let a simple but profound pedagogical technique go unused. Tell your students, "Jesus and Mary love you very much!"

It has been said that actions speak louder than words, which is very often true. But words that speak to one's heart and bring a listener into contact with the enormity of God's love have the ability to sink into the depth of our being and to change lives.

Remind your students today that they are loved, and while you're at it, remind yourself too.

Chuck Lamphier
St. Joseph Academy
Brownsville, Texas

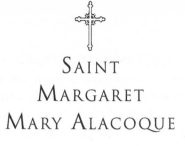

SAINT
MARGARET
MARY ALACOQUE

*It is only necessary to say energetically "I will"
and all will go well.*

As teachers, we say yes countless times each day. We say yes when asked to cover a class during our only planning period, and we say yes to coaching a sport we may know little about. Occasionally we even say yes when the campus minister asks us to sing selections from *The Little Mermaid* on the cafeteria stage during lunch. While such yesses sometimes seem insignificant, in each one we are ultimately saying yes to live as Christ for others. We are saying yes to self-giving love.

Knowing that we are called to this type of *agape* love through teaching is one thing, but actually living the gospel in the midst of fighting department members and freshmen who struggle to read is something completely different. It often seems that we are pushed beyond our breaking point as we try to follow Christ's example and fully give ourselves to others.

Saying yes is tiring. Saying yes makes us vulnerable, especially when we agree to something that is beyond our area of expertise. Sometimes it feels like we cannot force ourselves to utter another yes. But maybe that is what we need to do in order to fully be disciples of the risen Christ—to truly encounter God. Saying yes is our opportunity to participate in Christ's life, suffering, death, and resurrection. In saying yes, we live the paschal mystery.

Ultimately, we hope that by our example of constantly saying yes to live as Christ for others, our students will learn to say yes themselves. We hope that as they recognize their God-given dignity and realize their unique gifts and talents, they will not only remember to avoid "be" verbs in formal writing but—more important—to joyfully and selflessly give themselves for others. We pray that our students will always know and share God's inescapable love by constantly saying yes.

John Kyler
Moreau Seminary Postulant Program
Notre Dame, Indiana

Saint Marguerite Bourgeoys

Seeing Jesus in Our Students

Teaching is the work most suited to draw down the graces of God if it is done with purity of intention, without distinction between the poor and the rich, between relatives and friends and strangers, between the pretty and the ugly, the gentle and the grumblers, looking upon them all as drops of our Lord's blood.

Few experiences demand as much fine attention and control as encountering the Body and Blood of our Savior in the Eucharist. Like a jeweler setting a precious gem while sitting on the edge of a cliff, total focus must be on the treasure at hand. Each motion must be carefully considered and reevaluated in preparation for the next. Movements long lost to the void of habit suddenly seem to play out in painstaking slow motion. Mistakes are so costly, almost unthinkable.

So it is with our students. We are charged to treat each student—and especially as Marguerite challenged, all students—"as drops of our Lord's blood." This creates for us a momentous task.

In our teaching, we must pull apart the familiar tension between recognizing every student as fundamentally different and seeing every student as just the same. In their behaviors, learning styles, and backgrounds, no two students present the same teaching experience. We must prepare for, educate, and evaluate each one according to how God created him or her. At the same time, we must honor them all.

Marguerite laid down the challenge clearly: "without distinction."

Our busy lives and pressing needs tempt us to make distinctions, or to treat our pupils just the same without regard for their individual needs. To find the strength to be both impartial and fair, day in and day out, is to gain a greater understanding of God's plan for us and to experience God's grace.

And if we are called to "draw down the graces of God," as Marguerite concluded, it surely is not done for our own sake. By extending these same graces to our students, they will one day walk away from our care having learned how to hold others in their hands with as much honor and respect as we have held the Eucharist, "the drops of the Lord's blood."

Ricky Austin
St. Hilary Catholic School
Chicago, Illinois

SAINT MARY MACKILLOP

Do all you can with the means at your disposal, and calmly leave the rest to God.

These words from Australia's first saint ring true for school principals like me (even if you're not Australian, like I am!). Principals are often the budget setters, decision makers, visionaries, and spiritual leaders of their schools. Sometimes, constrained by our own budgets, we may also find ourselves the maintenance and janitorial workers. As principals, there is much that rests on our shoulders. What a comfort, then, is Mary MacKillop's invitation to "calmly leave the rest to God."

During Advent of my first year as a Catholic school principal, a mother came to my office because her family was unable to make payments on their utility bills. From the start of the year, I had been operating the school on a budget deficit. I was doing all I could to balance the budget, and I did not know what to do for this family.

I asked the pastor what we should do. He responded, "We will find the money somewhere." So we gave the family a check for enough money to cover the utility bills, plus some extra money for groceries.

The day after we wrote that check, a parishioner who knew nothing of this situation made a donation specifically earmarked "For a needy family in the school." The amount the parishioner gave was the same amount we had given to the school family.

As school leaders, we must model a faith that brings others to an encounter with God. As budget setters, school visionaries, and occasionally janitorial staff, we do whatever it takes and then leave room for God to work. Be calm, worry not, and trust in God's faithful provision.

Keiran Roche
St. John the Evangelist Catholic School
Tucson, Arizona

Saint Mary Magdalene

Surprised by Love

[Now Mary Magdalene stood outside the tomb crying.] Jesus said to her, "Woman, why are you weeping? Who are you looking for?" She thought it was the gardener and said to him, "Sir, if you carried him away, tell me where you laid him, and I will take him." Jesus said to her, "Mary!" She turned and said to him in Hebrew, "Rabbouni" which means Teacher. Jesus said to her, "Go to my brothers and tell them I am going to my Father and your Father, to my God and your God." Mary Magdalene hurried away and announced to the disciples, "I have seen the Lord!"

John 20:15–18

As teachers or administrators, we all have those days when we cannot wait for the dismissal bell to ring. One day in particular for me was just before Thanksgiving break during my first year of teaching. The fourth graders and I had had a particularly trying day and, come two thirty, our dismissal procedures fell apart. I realized that we would have to make a mad dash to the parking lot to stay on time for dismissal.

As I tried to hustle them out the door, exercising patience to not say "Hurry up!" for the umpteenth time, "Veronica" came up to me, gave me a big squeeze, and said, "Great day, Miss Seamon. I am thankful for you, and I love you."

Needless to say, my heart melted. The carpool line could wait! Then another student shouted, "*Yes!* Miss Seamon is giving out hugs today!" Every fourth grader proceeded to hug me on their way out the door saying, "I'm thankful for you, Miss Seamon, and I love you."

Just when I thought I had failed as a teacher, love entered. I saw the Lord that day in a very real, humbling, and powerful way—through the words and hugs of twelve ten-year-old children.

I have always had a special devotion to Mary Magdalene, the "Apostle to the Apostles" and "Beautiful Penitent." Mary is constantly surprised by the revelations of God's intimate and powerful love for her, which reinvigorates her to share the Gospel. Perhaps that's why Mary was the first to see Jesus after his Resurrection. Like me in the dismissal line, she was in haste to "finish up the details" after a day of certain failure: "Show me where his body is so I can take care of him."

Instead, she hears her name, uttered as if to say, "I'm thankful for you, Mary, and I love you." No wonder she ran to share the good news with the apostles.

May we, with Mary Magdalene, remain open to the surprising revelations of Christ's love for us. Then, renewed in our mission, may we proclaim with great joy at the end of the day—or even as break draws near—that we have seen the Lord!

Amy Wyskochil
Sacred Heart Interparochial School
Pinellas, Florida

Saint Maximilian Kolbe

Infinite Power

By obeying we raise ourselves beyond our little-ness and we can act in conformity with an infinite wisdom. . . . Through obedience we become infinitely powerful.

Auschwitz. The death camp turned museum remains a dark place, hopeless and sad, a per-petual reminder of the evil that humankind allowed to happen. Its message is memory, not hope. In a cell once used for executions, visitors see flowers, a candle, and a sober plaque—a quiet tribute to Maximilian Kolbe, a Catholic priest imprisoned there who chose to exchange his life for that of another prisoner. This obedience unto death was perfectly consistent with the rest of his life.

Working in education does nothing if not bring us face-to-face with our own littleness. We constant-ly question the wisdom of our decisions; we struggle against our powerlessness in the face of students' suf-fering and apathy. Every day, we find ourselves too small to teach the small to seek and love wisdom, too little to convince those little ones that they have power, strength, and a call to serve. God made us too small to do those things, but we can never be too small to obey the commands of our Father in heaven.

When Maximilian Kolbe died at Auschwitz, his death was one of millions. The significance of his death comes from the love that prompted his sacrifice. In the face of evil beyond comprehension, Maximilian did the unpleasant, agonizing, but utterly perfect will of God.

"The cross is the school of love," Maximilian once wrote, and the cross is in our schools, as it is everywhere. At every moment, God gives us ways to lay down our lives in love. Even in the face of a seemingly insurmountable evil, Maximilian Kolbe teaches us that, where we live as children of God, hope will not fail to survive.

Deandra Lieberman
St. Patrick-St. Vincent High School
Vallejo, California

Saint Patrick

*In 433 AD, on the eve of Easter Sunday, the
King of Tara decreed that no flame should be
lit before he lit his fire. Violators would forfeit
their lives. St. Patrick, however, celebrating the
Easter Vigil, blessed and enkindled the Paschal
Fire on the summit of the Hill of Slane for all to
see. When the King and his courtiers arrived at
Slane to confront Patrick, the saint explained
the light of the Paschal Mystery in terms they
could all understand. Moved to reverence, the
King granted Patrick permission to preach the
faith throughout Ireland.*

To enkindle hearts in a world grown chill," as J. R.
R. Tolkien famously instructed the elven lords in
The Lord of the Rings, is the vocation of the teacher. Our
singular vocation is to set the hearts and minds of our
students ablaze as they discover their own passions and
loves. As has been said, "Education is not the filling of
a pail, but the lighting of a fire."

Patrick simply did what all great teachers do: He
drew from the familiar images and experiences of his
milieu to reveal boldly and convincingly where God
is already present. Patrick's lighting of the Easter fire
to initiate the spring festival invited his onlookers to

experience their reality in a new and utterly life-transforming way.

Take the apostle Paul's admonition to his own student, Timothy, "to stir into flame the gift of God . . . the Spirit God has given us" (2 Tm 1:6–7). What a powerful image Paul provides us. The source of the flame is from God, and our vocation is to nurture and encourage that flame. We are not alone in doing this. It is the Spirit who works through each of us: teachers, coaches, mentors, parents, and siblings.

Patrick's challenge is our challenge: to keep the paschal fire burning brightly for all to see. So as we walk into our classrooms each day, let us pray, as the Irish would say, "Keep 'er lit!"

Fr. Sean McGraw, C.S.C.
Keough-Naughton Institute for Irish Studies
University of Notre Dame
Notre Dame, Indiana

Saint Paul

*God is able to make every grace abundant for
you, so that in all things, always having all
you need, you may have an abundance for
every good work.*

Children are truly a "gift from the Lord" (Ps 127:3).
Through them, God teaches us to be better people,
for children can be beautiful examples of grace and
the kindness, generosity, and love that flow from that
grace. This is the mystery of which Paul was always
aware and which fills his letters.

Recently, I asked a child who had just enrolled in
one of our Catholic schools what he liked best about his
new school. He said, "Everyone is so kind here, and I
love that." He reminded me that grace must always be
followed with kindness, no matter what the situation
may be. As the saying goes, "Be kind, for everyone you
meet is fighting a hard battle."

At another recent middle school visit, I sat down
with a boy to enjoy some leftover lasagna from the welcome lunch we had just served his teachers. As we ate,
he commented that it was the first time he had tried
lasagna. We chatted about his family and then, when
I saw that he had not eaten all of his meal, I asked if
he didn't like it. He responded, "I love it, but I want to

take the rest of it home so my grandmother can taste it, too." This young man reminded me that sharing one's gifts unselfishly is a true example of how grace includes generosity of spirit.

Not long ago, one very special teacher invited me to attend Mass with her in celebration of her mother's birthday. I was flattered but quickly brought to tears when she shared that her mother had passed away. I asked what her mother's name was, and she answered, "Grace." This young woman, with her deep affection for her faith and her mother, reminded me of the love that is inherent in grace. Thank God for the children and teachers in our lives who "bring us an abundance of grace for every good deed."

Rachel Moreno
ACE Service through Teaching
University of Notre Dame
Notre Dame, Indiana

Saint Philip Neri

Cheerfulness strengthens the heart and makes us try harder to have a good life; thus God's servants must always be in good spirits.

Philip Neri believed that faith and temperament are intimately connected, which leads me to think that he would have been an excellent high school teacher. I learned quickly in teaching that my mood would help to set the tone of my classroom. If I appeared irritated or tired, my students responded in turn by acting out. If I entered the room excited about religion, my temperament swayed the mood of the classroom to work with me. On rainy days in New Orleans or mornings after Mardi Gras parades, learning to put on a cheerful face was essential to classroom function.

I admired one teacher in particular for teaching me to practice constant cheer. "Mrs. King" experienced many trials in her personal and professional life but remained cheerful through it all. I watched her care for her sick mother for a year and mourn her eventual death and still raise three young children on a tight budget with great love. I observed her teach high school seniors the importance of living out their Christian vocations—lessons often met with distress, debate, and difficult questions—with grace and humor.

Occasionally, Mrs. King shared a personal struggle and asked for prayers but assured me still, "It'll be okay. God provides!" It was her mantra, and she managed to keep a smile on her face, greeting students in the hallway with, "Good morning, beautiful!" or entering her classroom belting out the song "We Are the World!"

Philip Neri noted, "Cheerfulness strengthens the heart and makes us try harder to have a good life, thus God's servants must always be in good spirits." Mrs. King taught me how trusting in God's grace and staying cheerful lifted her spirits and strengthened the hearts of those around her. May we pray to be cheerful servants of God and teach others to do likewise.

Allison Greene
Academy of Our Lady Catholic High School
New Orleans, Louisiana

BLESSED PIER GIORGIO FRASSATI

Verso l'alto!
("Toward the summit!")

Pier Giorgio Frassati is a wonderful modern role model for today's youth. Energetic, countercultural, faith-filled, athletic, and socially engaged, Frassati struggled as a student but earned a reputation for being drawn to highly strenuous physical activity. He loved long hikes, mountain climbing in the Italian Alps, and high-altitude skiing. On these expeditions, he was often heard to exclaim, *"Verso l'alto!"* ("Toward the summit!" or, more loosely translated, "Ever onward!")

Pier Giorgio's passion and commitment were always an inspiration to his friends and peers as he motivated them to keep going. *Verso l'alto*: Not a bad phrase to keep close at hand in our classrooms.

The Frassati family was wealthy and politically active. Pier Giorgio used the influence he had to fight fascist rule in his home country of Italy and to quietly tend to the needs of the poor in his native city of Torino. It is widely believed that his death at twenty-four was due to a virulent form of polio that he contracted from those he was trying to help. His family was stunned when large numbers of mourners, mostly strangers from the poor neighborhoods of Torino, showed up for his funeral Mass. He provides a witness for us to motivate and encourage every student with whom we are entrusted, especially the most challenged.

In photographs, Pier Giorgio Frassati doesn't look like a saint—more like a professional athlete or even a movie star. His dark hair, solid physique, broad shoulders, and generous smile made for an attractive countenance. His background, coming from a wealthy, politically connected family, would only have added to his mystique and desirability. Yet his passion was for the poor, for helping others become all that God made them to be, and always seeking what truly enhances and what brings society closer to perfection and to God. May we always strive for these same ideals in our classrooms with our students, encouraging them always: *Verso l'alto!*

Fr. Ronald Nuzzi
Renewing Identity, Strengthening Evangelization (RISE)
University of Notre Dame
Notre Dame, Indiana

Saint Rita of Cascia

The Good That God Wants

Rita of Cascia was born to an aged couple in fourteenth-century Italy. A deeply religious girl, she begged her parents at the age of twelve to allow her to become a nun. They refused, instead arranging a marriage to a rich and angry man embroiled in a violent family feud. Saddened that she could not enter the religious life, the young girl nevertheless committed herself to what she interpreted as God's will for her. According to popular tales, through her humility, kindness, and patience, Rita's husband eventually changed his ways, renouncing the feud and becoming a man of faith and prayer.

Sometimes the good we want is not the good God wants.

When I was a young mother, I was horrified to discover that my daughter Ruth had been assigned to a particular teacher one elementary school year. I worked with "Mr. Smith," so I knew about his penchant for sarcastic humor and his often caustic treatment of his students. His was a classroom—I was certain—that would not offer the nurture my girl needed. So I did what protective parents do (with apologies to school administrators everywhere): I begged the principal to reassign Ruth to another class. To no avail, the assignment stood. I was distraught.

Of course, I simply wanted what was good for my daughter. But as I fought on her behalf, I failed to consider that there were many things I did not, could not know about the year ahead—things only God knew that would reveal God's better plan.

I didn't know that Ruth would in fact flourish in Mr. Smith's classroom, that she would have the gumption to take his sarcasm in stride and speak up for herself when he turned caustic, or that she would have the insight to discover his tender side. I didn't know about Mr. Smith's tireless commitment to his students' success and his careful discernment of their gifts and potential. I did not know the significant role Mr. Smith would play in Ruth's academic and social development. It turned out to be her best year in elementary school.

The story might have ended differently. Ruth might have had a lousy year in Mr. Smith's class. Some experiences require years of hindsight before we can recognize God's hand at work. Indeed, Rita waited eighteen years for her husband to change. But her immediate, unwavering commitment to God's call suggests that she must have understood—at the ripe age of twelve—what took me many more years to learn. Sometimes the good we want is not the good God wants.

Ann Primus Berends
Education, Schooling, and Society
University of Notre Dame
Notre Dame, Indiana

SAINT SCHOLASTICA

*I asked you and you would not listen; so I
asked my God and he did listen.*

St. Scholastica was a nun and the twin sister of St. Benedict, the "father of Western monasticism." Though the two loved each other deeply, they saw each other only once a year at a house outside the monasteries where each of them lived.

On one of these visits, something prompted Scholastica to beg Benedict to stay and keep talking until daybreak. However, his Rule did not permit him to spend the night outside his monastery, and so he insisted he had to leave.

Undaunted, Scholastica bowed her head and asked God for help. Suddenly, such a strong thunderstorm came that Benedict could not leave. He asked her, "What have you done?" She replied, "I asked a favor of you, and you refused it. I asked it of God, and he has granted it." She had trusted God to provide the interruption she had so strongly desired.

Three days later, Scholastica died.

Upon learning of her death, Benedict gave thanks for that final extended visit, despite the interruption to his carefully planned schedule. Because of his sister's intuition, they had received from the hand of God an unexpected gift of time.

Many of us teachers like to plan out every minute of our classes. Then the announcements come on, five students are called to the office, and the fire alarm goes off. We never can be completely prepared for what will happen in the classroom on any particular day. No matter how well we craft our lesson plans, keep up on grading, get to know each student, and communicate with parents, the events of the day rarely go exactly as planned. We are working with people, after all. When life's unexpected interruptions discourage us, we can look to the example of Scholastica.

Interruptions can either discourage us or allow us to open ourselves more deeply to ways that God speaks to us. That fire drill may be an opportunity to hold the hand of a child you know is hurting. The last-minute call to recess duty may be the break you really needed from the classroom. That request for help with reshelving library books when you're ready to head home may lead to a conversation that enriches your day or someone else's.

May God help us embrace all the unplanned parts of our days through which—as the story of Scholastica and Benedict reminds us—God brings us closer to others and to him.

Andrea Novotney
Huntington Learning Centers
Madison, Wisconsin

Saint Sebastian

The devil strains every nerve to secure the souls
which belong to Christ. We should not grudge
our toil in wresting them from Satan and giving
them back to God.

Sports are the most popular childhood extracurricular activity in the United States, with forty million children participating each year. Yet one doesn't have to look deep into the world of youth and high school sports to see examples of competition tempting many away from godly behavior: A ribbon-clad soccer player deliberately yanks her opponent's ponytail, pulling her to the ground when the referee isn't looking. A mother swears from the sideline, "Are you blind, you #&** ref?!" A coach tells his most talented player to lie about his concussion to the trainer so the athlete can return to play in the championship game.

Sports provide a classroom for student athletes to learn virtue through their play: integrity, humility, teamwork, perseverance. Yet sports can also teach poor lessons: disrespect, dishonesty, selfishness. How can we as educators ensure that student athletes acquire moral character through their sport experiences? It all depends upon the environment we create and how coaches lead their teams.

127

Coach educators can look to Sebastian, the patron saint of athletes, for inspiration. Sebastian was known for his physical endurance and tirelessness and how it all focused on the end goal of spreading the Gospel. When the Roman army discovered Sebastian was a Christian, they shot him with arrows and left him for dead. Amazingly, he survived and carried on his mission to share the love of God. With Sebastian's strength and courage, we must be champions for every child's right to play sports in a safe, secure, fun, and nurturing environment—a godly environment freed from the toxic forces that have become normalized in our current culture of youth sports. With the love of God, we must toil for the souls of all athletes.

Kristin Komyatte Sheehan
Play Like a Champion Today
University of Notre Dame
Notre Dame, Indiana

Saint Teresa Benedicta of the Cross (Edith Stein)

A Teacher's Legacy

The nation doesn't simply need what we have.
It needs what we are.

Not long ago, I was with my eighth-grade students visiting a high school that many of our St. Patrick's graduates attend. "Howard," an accomplished senior and former student, stopped me in the hall during the tour. "Do you have a minute?" he asked. "I want to tell you about a revelation I just had."

He said that, at a recent Sunday Mass, he noticed as he looked around that many of his former elementary school classmates were present, which made him realize that they are all actively practicing their faith. As he thought about it further, he realized that several other elementary classmates were involved in service, mission trips, and significant leadership roles at their current high school. He said, "I guess I wanted to tell you that you and St. Patrick played an important role in that. You did a really good job of preparing us. Thank you!"

Besides being one of those sacred moments that makes teaching so rewarding, Howard's revelation confirmed for me the power and timely insight of Teresa Benedicta's words, which burst with urgency and challenge. It is our privilege to reveal the truth of the Gospel message and the social teachings of our Church that shout, "You are enough! Live boldly and wholeheartedly. Your families, your communities, our church, and our world need your gifts!"

This message must be stronger than the contradictory messages bombarding our students. We must take advantage of the time we have to tell them God's version of who they are. It must be infused in every aspect of our school community and culture. Howard and his classmates believed the message our school community was entrusted to share with them. As a result, they are living wholeheartedly, and their generosity of time and talent is blessing others. Thus, our students become the very fulfillment of Edith Stein's vision: They become precisely what our world needs.

Colleen Santoni
St. Patrick Catholic School
Dallas, Texas

SAINT TERESA OF AVILA

*Accustom yourself continually to make many
acts of love, for they enkindle and melt the soul.*

Teresa of Avila is a study in apparent contradictions: a mystical pragmatist, simultaneously radical and obedient. As a child, she recruited her brother to run away in hope of becoming martyred by the Moors. (They didn't make it far. Their uncle brought them home.) Many stories attributed to her reveal a woman of deep and abiding faith—and just a touch of sass.

In one account, on her way to a sick friend's bedside, the distraught nun was thrown off her horse into a river. Soaked and furious, Teresa shouted at God, "If this is how you treat your friends, no wonder you have so few!"

In another memorable story, a gift of food arrived at the convent during a time appointed for penance. She ordered it to be prepared, saying, "There is a time for penance and a time for partridge."

Her strength of personality powered monumental work. She founded the Discalced Carmelites, established dozens of convents and cloisters, and penned spiritual writings that earned her the designation of Doctor of the Church—the first woman to receive that title.

131

Teresa's storied life balanced obedience and responsiveness; she cultivated a relationship with Christ through prayer and retreat and made Christ known to others through fearless and demanding acts of love.

As teachers, we can run orderly classrooms and provide competent instruction without fulfilling our obligation to love our students. Likewise, classrooms can be filled with warmth and easy sentiments without meeting the defining characteristic of our ministry—to teach. Our self-giving must always both comfort and challenge the students entrusted to us. Like Teresa, we stand in the space where the mystical meets the practical. May some portion of her stalwart spirit be within us as we strive to make our classrooms places where children come to know their Creator by learning about creation and as we provide an education that enables them to see the world and themselves imbued with dignity, goodness, and purpose by a God who knows and loves us.

Andrea Cisneros
Notre Dame ACE Academies
Tucson, Arizona, and Tampa, Florida

BLESSED TERESA OF CALCUTTA

PENCILS IN GOD'S HAND

I don't claim anything of the work. It's his work. I'm like a little pencil in his hand. That's all. He does the thinking. He does the writing. The pencil has nothing to do with it. The pencil has only to be allowed to be used. In human terms, the success of our work should not have happened, no? That is a sign that it's his work, and that he is using others as instruments—all our Sisters. None of us could produce this. Yet see what he has done.

In my fifth year of teaching, I had a realization that completely changed the way I approach teaching. On the morning before a particularly busy day, I stopped in the school chapel for a few minutes of silence. And in the quiet I realized, "It is God who has allowed me to get up this morning. Without God's willing it, I could not take another breath, could not remain standing in the front of the classroom, could not open my mouth to speak." I saw that everything—from my enthusiasm for the work, to my pedagogical skills, to my ability to connect with young children—is God's gift and could be gone in an instant. I recognized that the power to be an effective teacher does not rest with me.

How many times have I rushed around, often chaotically, trying in a hundred ways to make my teaching excellent, "too busy" to spend dedicated time with God each day? How ironic. Anything good I have ever done for the students has come entirely from him, yet I worried and hurried as if I were in control.

As Mother Teresa taught her sisters, the true way to serve is the opposite of being too busy. It is taking the time each day to nurture our own relationships with God. This means setting aside a time for silence and prayer, as well as slowing down enough to notice his presence throughout the day.

God does not need teachers who work wonders for students in their own power. God needs teachers who realize that they are nothing without him and who humbly place themselves in his service each day. God needs empty vessels, ready for his use. The best teachers are those who turn their classrooms over to Christ the Teacher. They are nothing but pencils in his hand.

Mary DeMott
Holy Spirit Preparatory School
Atlanta, Georgia

SAINT THEODORA GUERIN

BEARING AND FORBEARING

You may have to wait longer than you would like, you may have to bear privations; but, bear and forebear. Have confidence in the Providence that so far has never failed us. The way is not yet clear. Grope along slowly. Do not press matters; be patient, be trustful.

Shortly after I started my work as a professor of education, I sat in the back of a poorly equipped classroom in New Orleans, watching a first-year teacher trying to teach. I was surprised that she was doing so poorly in front of her students, especially because I had reviewed her lesson plans multiple times and they were among some of the best I had ever read.

As I watched the class, I saw students throwing things, leaving their seats, and otherwise creating chaos. The teacher recognized how rough things were. I could see that she was on the verge of tears just a few minutes into her lesson, but she kept going. She kept correcting off-task and inappropriate behaviors, and she kept insisting that the students follow her plans and not their own. Finally her tears spilled over, and my heart broke for her. She was doing everything in her control to have the best class possible while many, many things still went wrong.

When the students left her room, the teacher wept for several minutes and then asked, "How do I make it so they can learn in here?" We talked about breaking things into smaller parts, setting smaller expectations for her students' behaviors and learning, and then celebrating lots of little milestones. The teacher was determined to do right by her students.

When I returned to her classroom three weeks later, things were improving. By the time I returned in the spring, things had turned around! She was running the class efficiently, students were learning, and the classroom had a pure and simple joy that was palpable to all.

It is perhaps not surprising that this teacher, who clearly had the virtues of forbearance and patience from the beginning, is still a teacher today. She starts the school year slowly and builds each class with small steps. Being a great teacher is much like surrendering ourselves to God's will: "Bear and forebear. Have confidence. . . . Be patient, be trustful."

Brian S. Collier
ACE Service through Teaching
University of Notre Dame
Notre Dame, Indiana

SAINT THÉRÈSE OF LISIEUX

*Even when I have nothing to offer God . . . then
I will give God this nothing.*

It was seven thirty on a Monday morning and so cold I could see my breath—in Texas! A sprawling line of shivering middle school children stretched before me. When the bell signaled the time for morning prayers, a bold eighth grader said what we were all thinking: "It's too cold! Can we just pray inside?"

Without missing a beat, the middle school matron proclaimed, "Offer it up!" This simple phrase—three little words for facing adversity—became a golden thread woven into the tapestry of my early teaching years, reminding me of Thérèse and her self-surrendering way of ministry to others.

What does it mean to offer it up? Are you scrambling to finish lesson plans on Sunday night before Monday's due date? Offer it up! Exhausted after a full day of teaching, tutoring, coaching, or surprise-parent-teacher-conferencing but on duty for preparing dinner tonight? Offer it up! Feeling the joy of that student's lightbulb moment but sorry for so little time to celebrate it? Offer it up.

They are simple words to say but sometimes frustrating to hear and act upon when trapped in the beautiful mess thirty students bring into a classroom. In those moments, St. Thérèse's model of surrender offers helpful insight.

When we trust God completely with every joy and struggle and go to God with open arms, as children to a parent, every "offer it up" becomes a turning point, changing every task to an offering of prayer. "Offering it up" focuses us on what we have to give. Some days that is simply nothing. But Thérèse reminds us that it is in the nothings that our deepest prayers translate into the greatest three words of trust we can say to Christ and to those in our care each day: I love you.

Abigail Salazar
Little Flower Catholic School
Mobile, Alabama

Saint Thomas Aquinas

The Beginning of Glory in Us

*Eternal life is the perfect fulfillment of desire . . .
because whatsoever is delightful will be there
superabundantly.*

"Mr. Graff, when your dog dies, does he go to
heaven?"

Great. How was I to explain to a group of eight-
year-olds why they won't see their pets in heaven?
The eternal third-grade teacher dilemma arose: Should
I divert their attention with a well-placed anecdote or
actually answer the question?

Luckily, in my third-grade class, we always know
who to go to for answers: the patron saint of students
and Doctor of the Church, Thomas Aquinas. I responded, "Well, St. Thomas said that you will have everything
you need to be perfectly happy in heaven. So, if you
really need your dog to be truly happy in heaven, he'll
be there." *Whew. Okay, next question!*

"Who am I and where do I come from?"

"Are angels real?"

"If God knew that people would do bad things, why
did he create them in the first place?"

"Where did God come from?"

It takes a surprising amount of theology to answer
third graders' religion questions accurately. My

students have challenged me to view the world through spiritually inquisitive eyes. They look upon the world and see God's infinite majesty everywhere on display. Their curiosity knows no bounds, and their questions reveal a deep desire to know more completely the God of their lives, a God who loved them into existence and asks for that same love in return.

A life of faith is born of questions and grows in response to the answers of love we give through our lives. When Christ invites us to "Come and see," he always awaits our response. Come and see the beauty that pours through eyes of faith. Like children, come and behold a world lit by eternity. "Grace," wrote St. Thomas, "is nothing else than a beginning of glory in us."

Patrick Graff
Incarnation Catholic Elementary School
St. Petersburg, Florida

SAINT THOMAS MORE

*Sir Thomas More: "Why not be a teacher?
You'd be a fine teacher, perhaps a great one."*

Richard Rich: "If I was, who would know it?"

*Sir Thomas More: "You, your pupils, your
friends, God. Not a bad public, that."*

M r. Clary, you are *still* a nerd!"
So said one of my seventh-grade students during my second year of teaching in Mobile, Alabama, after I revealed that I was a nerd in high school. As laughter filled the classroom, it was clear that everyone in the class (myself included!) knew that this student had spoken the truth.

One of the great lessons to be taken from the life of Thomas More, as depicted in Robert Bolt's 1966 movie *A Man for All Seasons*, is the virtue of knowing the truth humbly and living it out courageously. I have confronted many instances in teaching when living the truth was often a hardship—having a difficult conversation with a parent, maintaining some semblance of professionalism during the heat of a competitive basketball game, or even how I described my experience of teaching to my family, housemates, and friends.

141

Once my classroom doors closed, though, "the truth" stopped being an inconvenience and became a mountain that my students and I scaled (or attempted to scale!) together. The most joy-filled moments in the classroom were those "aha moments" when, after some hard work and coaxing, something would suddenly click in a student's mind. A piece of truth had been revealed; a slope of the mountain conquered.

God's truth surrounds us always and encompasses all things. What an amazing and noble gift we teachers have been given to play a part in—making even a fraction of that truth accessible to our students. Each time this happens, whether through equations, conjugations, timelines, or chemical reactions, the disproportionate joy we receive is a reminder of the importance of the work entrusted to us, the blessing of making visible what was hidden as a seed. As Robert Bolt's Thomas More insists, we share that sublime joy, that sacramental moment when some knowledge about God's world illuminates the mind and heart, with our pupils, our friends, and perhaps most incredibly, with God—"not a bad public, that!"

Drew Clary
Most Pure Heart of Mary Catholic School
Mobile, Alabama

Saint Veronica Giuliani

*I came to myself with these precise words:
nothing will be able to separate me from the
will of God, neither anxieties, nor sorrows nor
toil nor contempt nor temptation nor creatures
nor demons nor darkness, not even death itself,
because, in life and in death, I want all, and in
all things, the will of God.*

In reading this quote by Veronica Giuliani, my first reaction is, "What utter selflessness and deep insight this woman possessed. She would have been a teacher with an extremely high bar of expectations!"

Upon further reflection, however, I see that Veronica's words reveal less about her and more about the powerful mystery and glory of God. What kind of visions inspired Veronica to have this burning determination, this consuming thirst, this tenacious refusal to allow anything to separate her from the will of God?

As she recorded in her journal, her visions of Christ were consummate revelations of God's love as seen in Christ's suffering. They led her to risk everything and join Christ in his physical and emotional pain. Though initially Veronica shrank from this path—a hesitation that gives me hope that I can overcome my own doubts and fears and make God's will my life's purpose—she finally leapt in faith and surrendered completely to God.

Each of us has glimpsed a reflection—in our own lives, in our students' lives—of what Veronica recognized so clearly. The God who shaped the mountains and formed the seas, who took on the human body he designed, who suffered on our behalf, this God wants to be personally and intimately at the center of each of our lives. Continually, we strive to surrender our will to our Creator and to invite our students to do the same. Though we may sometimes procrastinate and become busy with our responsibilities in school, Veronica challengingly teaches that only the act of surrendering every minute of every day to the total will of God results in the transformation we all desire.

Donna Frazier
Saint Francis Xavier School
Taos, Missouri

Saint Vincent de Paul

The educator and those being educated learn mutually, where teachers not only evangelize but are evangelized by the poor. Contemporary documents note that persons must not only be the objects of formation, they must be subjects within the formation process.

Vincent inspires us to see Christ particularly in relationship with those in need. Within our schools, many of us encounter families who cannot afford the necessary resources for their children or students who are below grade level for a host of reasons not of their own choosing. Whether it is educational support, basic physical needs, emotional stability, or a spiritual foundation, they need help, and we want to provide it.

And yet, if we simply assume that, when we share our goods and services, those we serve have nothing to share with us in return—that giving is a one-way street—we find that our emotional resources are quickly depleted. On the other hand, if we pay attention and listen, we soon see how much people in need also have to share. We begin to realize that true *religion*—and true *education*, as Vincent defined it—is found among the poor.

I was blessed to work in a school community that strove to break the cycle of poverty. The school took initiative in preparing students for lifelong academic success and achievement. It was exciting work, but needless to say, I departed school each day quite exhausted.

On my way to the parking lot, however, I always had a pleasant encounter with the grandmother of some of our students. She sold snacks out of a shopping cart for a couple of hours each afternoon. Her warm demeanor encouraged families to linger after they made their purchases. It became routine for me to wave in greeting and say, "*Hasta luego . . . que te vaya bien.*" ("Hope all goes well for you.")

Her response always spoke to my heart: "*Primero Dios.*" ("If God wills it.")

I was humbled by this woman's faith and hope in God under all circumstances. She did not live her life in fear despite the tribulations she faced. With two simple words, *primero Dios*, she became my encounter with Christ. Here is a lesson for all teachers to remember: True education is not only to evangelize but to be evangelized by the poor.

April Michelle García
Onward Readers
Los Angeles, California

ABOUT THE ALLIANCE FOR CATHOLIC EDUCATION

The Alliance for Catholic Education (ACE), housed in the Institute for Educational Initiatives at the University of Notre Dame, exists for one purpose: to strengthen and sustain Catholic schools. This close-knit, multigenerational program—honored by the White House, emulated by other universities, and growing in its impact and spectrum of services—engages people who are passionate about meeting the needs of under-resourced elementary and secondary schools around the globe. Over the years, the program has become one of Notre Dame's best known "exports"— it can be found in hundreds of US schools, dozens of Catholic dioceses, and several foreign countries.

ACE began in 1993 as a two-year service program (now called ACE Service through Teaching) that offered committed and successful college graduates the opportunity to serve as full-time teachers in under-resourced Catholic schools. Because good teachers need excellent formation, ACE prepares its teachers in an innovative Master of Education program at Notre Dame, which brings them to campus for two summers of intensive training and sends them out into classrooms during the

147

school year. These teachers represent a broad variety of undergraduate disciplines with a diverse set of backgrounds and experiences. While teaching, they live in small communities of four to seven members and are supported throughout the year by both pastoral and academic staff at Notre Dame. One of the program's priorities is that ACE teachers develop their professional skills and personal spirituality in the context of community, sharing with one another the journey of becoming committed Catholic school teachers.

ACE Service through Teaching has spawned numerous kindred programs by responding to emerging needs within and surrounding Catholic schools. These include: formation for teachers and administrators who seek to become principals or licensed in English as a New Language or Teaching Exceptional Children; professional services that are customized to help Catholic schools confront challenges such as participating in federal grant programs and strengthening curriculum and instruction; and outreach opportunities that galvanize all sorts of Catholic school supporters who want to collaborate in addressing key concerns. Timely subjects for a growing grid of efforts include parental choice advocacy, urgent educational trends both local and global, and increasing access for Latino children and their families in US Catholic education.

The work of ACE to confront today's challenges in Catholic schools is enhancing lives all around. And as the program's growing number of graduates and advocates like to say, "We're just getting started!"

RESOURCES

Opening Quote

Christian Classics Ethereal Library. "V. The Real Life of Saint Thomas." Accessed March 17, 2014. http://www.ccel.org/ccel/chesterton/aquinas.vii.html.

Saint Albert the Great (The Importance of Questions)

D. J. Kennedy. Jacques Maritain Center. "Albertus Magnus." Accessed March 17, 2014. http://www3.nd.edu/Departments/Maritain/etext/albert.htm.

Saint Alberto Hurtado (Reynolds, Serving Our "Little Bosses")

Martin, S.J., James. "St. Alberto Hurtado, S.J." *America: In All Things*. Last modified August 18, 2010. http://americamagazine.org/node/126605.

Saint Alberto Hurtado (Faas, Becoming Authentic Lessons)

Faith of the Fathers Saint Quote. "Saint Quote—Saint Alberto Hurtado Cuchaga." Posted March 23, 2007. http://faithofthefatherssaintquote.blogspot.com/2007/03/saint-quote-saint-alberto-hurtado.html.

Saint Aloysius Gonzaga (A Powerful Humility)

Defend the Faith: Catholic Quotes. Accessed March 17, 2014. http://www.angelfire.com/nb/defendthefaith/quotes.html.

Saint Alphonsus Liguori (Daily Perseverance)

Hammer, Rev. Bonaventure. In *Mary, Help of Christians and the Fourteen Saints Invoked as Holy Helpers, Part VI*. Released

August 31, 2010. https://archive.org/stream/maryhelpof-
christ33596gut/pg33596.txt.

Saint Ambrose (Whatever It Takes)

Omera, Ferguson, et al. *Revitalizing Catholic Schools*. Released
January 4, 2012. http://www.omearaferguson.com/files/
RevitalizingCatholicSchools.pdf.

Saint André Bessette (Carlin, A Saint at the Door)

Congregation of Holy Cross: United States Province of Priests
and Brothers. "About St. André Bessette." Accessed March 17,
2014. http://www.holycrossusa.org/spirituality/saint-andre/
about-st-andre-bessette.

Saint André Bessette (Morgan, Brushes of Grace)

American Catholic. "Saint of the Day." Posted January 6,
2014. http://www.americancatholic.org/features/saints/
saint.aspx?id=1252.

Saint Angela Merici (Inspired Surprises)

St. Angela Merici Writings (Counsels, Prologue 15, 17–18).
Accessed March 17, 2014. http://ursulinesmsj.org/_uploads/
SaintAngelaMericiwritings.pdf.

Saints Anne and Joachim (Preparing the Gifts to Come)

Catholic News Agency. "Sts. Anne and Joachim." Accessed
March 17, 2014. http://www.catholicnewsagency.com/saint.
php?n=313.

Saint Augustine of Hippo (Wolohan, Praying with Hope)

Christian Classics Ethereal Library. *Confessions of Saint Augustine*, Chapter XI. Accessed March 17, 2014. http://www.ccel.org/ccel/augustine/confess.iv.xi.html#iv.xi-p0.2.

Saint Augustine of Hippo (Kirkland, Simply Love)

Catholic Doors. "Prayer of St. Augustine of Hippo: Love and Do What You Will." Accessed March 18, 2014. www.catholic-doors.com/prayers/english/p05010.htm.

Blessed Basil Moreau (The Mystery Within)

Moreau, Blessed Basil. Circular Letter 36, April 15, 1849. Holy Cross Institute. Accessed March 18, 2014. http://www.holycrossinstitute.org/sites/default/files/u11/from_the_writings_of_father_moreau.pdf.

Hopkins, G. M. Poetry Foundation, Poems & Prose. "God's Grandeur." Accessed March 18, 2014. http://www.poetryfoundation.org/poem/173660.

Saint Benedict of Nursia (Vereecke, Our Shared Mission)

Christian Classics Ethereal Library. *Holy Rule of St. Benedict*, Chapter LXIV. Accessed March 18, 2014. http://www.ccel.org/ccel/benedict/rule.lxvi.html.

Saint Benedict of Nursia (Torigian, Listening by Heart)

Christian Classics Ethereal Library. *Holy Rule of St. Benedict*, Prologue. http://www.ccel.org/ccel/benedict/rule.ii.html.

Saint Bernadette Soubirous (*Vita, Dulcedo, et Spes*)

McEachern, Patricia. *A Holy Life: The Writings of Saint Bernadette of Lourdes*. San Francisco: Ignatius Press, 2000, p. 29.

Saint Catherine of Siena (Mayotte, Lose Yourself in the Cross)

Scudder, Vida Dutton (Trans., Ed.) "Saint Catherine of Siena as Seen in Her Letters." London, New York: J. M. Dent and E. P. Dutton, 1905. Drawn by Love. http://www.drawnbylove.com/Scudder%20letters.htm#2Daniella3.

Saint Catherine of Siena (Fennell, A Time to Endure)

Scudder, Vida Dutton (Trans., Ed.) "Saint Catherine of Siena as Seen in Her Letters." London, New York: J. M. Dent and E. P. Dutton, 1905. The Integrated Catholic Life. http://www.integratedcatholiclife.org/tag/st-catherine-of-siena.

Venerable Catherine McAuley (Caring the "Parent Way")

Religious Sisters of Mercy, Rules and Constitutions, Section 148. Internet Archive—Catholic Theological Union. Accessed March 18, 2014. http://archive.org/stream/rulesconstitutio00sist#page/148/mode/1up.

Servant of God Dorothy Day (The Assurance of Community)

Day, Dorothy. *The Long Loneliness*. New York: Harper & Row, 1952, p. 243.

Saint Elizabeth Ann Seton (Daily Gardening)

Vincentian Online Library. "Spiritual Gems of Elizabeth Ann Seton." Accessed March 18, 2014. http://famvin.org/wiki/Category:Spiritual_Gems_of_Elizabeth_Ann_Seton.

Saint Francis de Sales (Learning by Doing)

Christian Classics Ethereal Library. "Introduction to the Devout Life." Accessed March 18, 2014. http://www.ccel.org/ccel/desales/devout_life.html.

Saint Francis of Assisi (Paying Attention)

Chesterton, G.K. *St. Francis of Assisi*, Nashville: TerodeDesign, 1924, p. 47.

Browning, E.B. (1917). "86. From 'Aurora Lee'". Nicholson and Lee, eds., Oxford Book of Mystical Verse. Bartleby.com at http://www.bartleby.com/236/86.html.

Blessed Frederic Ozanam (When Faith Is Challenged)

Ramson, Fr. Ronald. The Word Among Us. "Giving the Gift of Self: The Inspiring Stewardship Story of Blessed Frederic Ozanam." http://www.ascensioncatholic.net/TOPICS/parish/stewardship/GivingGiftOfSelf.html.

Venerable Archbishop Fulton J. Sheen (The Power of the Rosary)

Renew America. "Archbishop Sheen Today!—Praying the Rosary." Posted September 8, 2004. http://www.renewamerica.com/columns/kralis/040918.

Saint Ignatius of Loyola (Bambrick, The Gift of Reflection)

St. Ignatius. "Letter #48 'To Father Alfonso Román, On the Spiritual Value of Contradictions.' July 14, 1556." *Letters and Writings of St. Ignatius Loyola*, Woodstock Theological Center at Georgetown University. http://woodstock.georgetown.edu/ignatius/letter48.htm.

Saint Ignatius of Loyola. *Autobiography of St. Ignatius*, Subsections 5–8. Project Gutenberg. Released February 6, 2008. http://www.gutenberg.org/ebooks/24534.

Saint Ignatius of Loyola (Gomez, Whole Surrender)

Christian Classics Ethereal Library. "Spiritual Exercises of St. Ignatius of Loyola, Contemplation to Gain Love." Accessed March 18, 2014. http://www.ccel.org/ccel/ignatius/exercises.xvi.html.

Saint Ignatius of Loyola (Carey, *Ad Majorem Dei Gloriam*)

Ferrell, S.J, Allen P. *The Jesuit Ratio Studiorum of 1599*. Boston College Library. Accessed March 18, 2014. http://www.bc.edu/sites/libraries/ratio/ratio1599.pdf.

Saint Irenaeus of Lyons (To Be Fully Alive)

Christian Classics Ethereal Library. "The Apostolic Fathers with Justin Martyr and Irenaeus." St. Irenaeus. Against Heresies, Book IV, Chapter 20, Part 7. Accessed March 18, 2014. http://www.ccel.org/ccel/schaff/anf01.ix.vi.xxi.html.

Saint Isaac Jogues (Grace to Overcome)

Eternal World Television Network. "Saint Isaac Jogues, Martyr." *Lives of Saints*, John J. Crawley & Co., Inc. Accessed March 18, 2014. http://www.ewtn.com/library/mary/jogues.htm.

Saint John Baptist de La Salle (Ambassadors for Christ)

Loes, Augustine, FSC, and Francis Huether, FSC (editors). *The Complete Works of Saint John Baptist de La Salle*. Richard Arnandez, FSC, and Augustine Loes, FSC (translators), Lasallian Publications, 1994, 195.2. Accessed March 18, 2014.

http://lasallian.info/wp-content/uploads/2012/12/Meditations-2007.pdf.

Saint John Bosco (O'Donnell, Escaping the Anger Trap)

Bosco, John (1884). An exhortation to educators, Rome, May 10, 1884, MBVII, p. 231. Informal Education Archives. Accessed March 18, 2014. http://www.infed.org/archives/christian_youthwork/bosco_exhortation_to_educators.htm.

Saint John Bosco (Brands, A Just Cause)

SaintBosco.Org, "Quotes from St. John Bosco (533)." Accessed March 19, 2014. http://saintbosco.org/quotes/index.php?offset = 340.

Marshall, James. *Miss Nelson is Missing!* New York: Houghton Mifflin, 1977.

Saint John Bosco (Reynolds, The Power of Persuasion)

Excerpts from Epistolario, Torino 1959 (4) 201–203. "Readings for the Feast of St. John Bosco." Liturgies.Net. Accessed March 19, 2014. http://www.liturgies.net/saints/donbosco/readings.htm.

Blessed John Henry Newman (True Affirmation)

Newman Reader. "A Short Visit to the Blessed Sacrament before Meditation." The National Institute for Newman Studies. Accessed March 19, 2014. http://www.newmanreader.org/works/meditations/meditations9.html.

Merton, Thomas. *New Seeds of Contemplation.* ©Abbey of Gethsemani, New York: New Directions, 1961, p. 31.

Saint John of the Cross (Silence)

Kavanaugh, Kieran OCD, and Otilio Rodriguez, OCD (translators) (1991). *The Collected Works of St. John of the Cross* (Letter 20). Washington, DC: ICS Publications, p. 20.

Saint John Paul II (Be Not Afraid)

Perth Catholic Youth Ministry. "Blessed Pope John Paul II: Love." Accessed March 19, 2014. http://cym.com.au/spirituality/inspirational-quotes/blessed-pope-john-paul-ii.

Saint John the Baptist (Called to Action)

St. Joseph Edition of the *New American Bible*, Luke 3:3–4, 12. New York: Catholic Book Publishing Corp., p. 103.

Saint John Vianney (On Collective Prayer)

Poust, Mary. *The Essential Guide to Catholic Prayer and the Mass.* New York: Penguin, 2011, p. 22.

Saint Joseph, Father of Jesus (Saint Joseph's Lantern)

St. Joseph Edition of the *New American Bible*, Luke 2:4–5. New York: Catholic Book Publishing Corp., p. 100.

Saint Joseph of Cupertino (The Flying Saint)

Goodier, S.J., Alban. "St. Joseph of Cupertino: The Dunce." Saints for Sinners. Eternal World Television Network. Accessed March 19, 2014. http://www.ewtn.com/library/mary/joseph.htm.

Saint Juan Diego Cuauhtlatoatzin (Eyes on the Goal)

Vatican News Service. "Juan Diego Cuauhtlatoatzin." Accessed March 19, 2014. http://www.vatican.va/news_services/liturgy/saints/ns_lit_doc_20020731_juan-diego_en.html.

Saint Julie Billiart (Respect Your Children)

Books Now. John M. Kelly Library. *The Life of Blessed Julie Billiart*. Accessed March 19, 2014. http://booksnow2.scholarsportal.info/ebooks/oca1/34/lifeofjuliebilla00unknuoft/lifeofjuliebilla00unknuoft_djvu.txt.

Saint Katharine Drexel (The Gift of This Moment)

"A Spiritual Journey Experience with St. Katharine Drexel 15." Posted January 5, 2012. http://ajourneywithstkatharine.blogspot.com/search?updated-max = 2012-01-05T19:33:00-05:00&max-results = 7&start = 7&by-date = false.

Saint Laura Montoya (Meeting Them Where They Are)

Vatican News Service. "Laura Montoya." Accessed March 19, 2014. http://www.vatican.va/news_services/liturgy/saints/ns_lit_doc_20040425_montoya_sp.html.

Saint Lawrence (A Time to Laugh)

Catholic Exchange. "Saint Lawrence." Posted August 10, 2013. http://catholicexchange.com/st-lawrence.

Gerloff, Pamela, EdD. "Are You Meeting Your Laugh Quota? Why You Should Laugh Like a 5-Year-Old." *Psychology Today*. Posted June 21, 2011. http://www.psychologytoday.com/blog/the-possibility-paradigm/201106/are-you-meeting-your-laugh-quota-why-you-should-laugh-5-year-ol.

Saint Luke (Seeing Faith with Fresh Eyes)

St. Joseph Edition of the *New American Bible*, Luke 5:26. New York: Catholic Book Publishing Corp., p. 107.

Saint Marcellin Champagnat (Brandt, Becoming Nothing for God)

Champagnat.org. "Letters of Marcellin, 001, 1-12-1893." Accessed March 19, 2014. http://www.champagnat.org/510. php?a = 2b&id = 1343&cat = 1.

Saint Marcellin Champagnat (Lamphier, Say It Aloud)

Champagnat.org. "Letters of Marcellin, 014, 21/01/1830." Accessed March 19, 2014. http://www.champagnat.org/510. php?a = 2b&id = 1358&cat = 1.

Saint Margaret Mary Alacoque (Modeling a Joyful Yes)

Guiley, Rosemary. *The Quotable Saint*. New York: Visionary Living, 2002, p. 298.

Saint Marguerite Bourgeoys (Seeing Jesus in Our Students)

Bourgeoys, Marguerite. *The Writings of Marguerite Bourgeoys: Autobiography and Spiritual Testament*. Montreal: Musée Marguerite-Bourgeoys, p. 201.

Saint Mary MacKillop (God's Generous Provision)

MaryMacKillop.org. "Letters of Mary MacKillop." Accessed March 19, 2014. http://www.marymackillop.org.au/marys-story/beginnings.cfm?loadref = 2.

Saint Mary Magdalene (Surprised by Love)

St. Joseph Edition of the *New American Bible*, John 20:15–18. New York: Catholic Book Publishing Corp., p. 176.

Saint Maximilian Kolbe (Infinite Power)

The Integrated Catholic Life. "Daily Catholic Quote: Maximilian Kolbe." Posted August 14, 2013. http://www.integratedcatholiclife.org/tag/st-maximilian-kolbe.

Saint Patrick (Lighting Fires)

SacredFire.net. "St. Patrick and the Arrival of Christianity." Accessed March 19, 2014. http://www.sacredfire.net/celt-christ.html.

Unknown quote typically attributed to WB Yeats, but no proof. Read more at http://www.irishtimes.com/news/education/education-is-not-the-filling-of-a-pail-but-the-lighting-of-a-fire-it-s-an-inspiring-quote-but-did-wb-yeats-say-it-1.1560192?page = 2.

Saint Paul (Examples of Grace)

St. Joseph Edition of the *New American Bible*, 2 Corinthians 9:8. New York: Catholic Book Publishing Corp., p. 277. (& confirm)

Saint Philip Neri (Cheerful Living)

Faber, Frederick William (Trans.). "The Maxims and Sayings of Phillip Neri." Accessed March 19, 2014. http://en.wikisource.org/wiki/The_maxims_and_sayings_of_St_Philip_Neri.

Blessed Pier Giorgio Frassati (Ever Onward)

Frassati USA. "A Saint on Skis." Accessed March 19, 2014. http://www.frassatiusa.org/index.cfm?load = page&page = 301&category = 1.

Saint Rita of Cascia (The Good That God Wants)

Catholic Online. "Saints & Angels: St. Rita." Accessed March 21, 2014. http://www.catholic.org/saints/saint.php?saint_id = 205.

Saint Scholastica (The Blessing of Interruptions)

American Catholic. "Saint of the Day." Posted February 10, 2014. http://www.americancatholic.org/features/saints/saint.aspx?id=1287.

Saint Sebastian (Sporting Virtue)

New Advent. "St. Sebastian." Accessed March 21, 2014. http://www.newadvent.org/cathen/13668a.htm.

**Saint Teresa Benedicta of the Cross (Edith Stein)
(A Teacher's Legacy)**

Garcia, Laura. Catholic Education Resource Center. "Edith Stein—Convert, Nun, Martyr." Crisis 15, no. 6, 32–35. Accessed March 21, 2014. http://www.catholiceducation.org/articles/religion/re0001.html.

Saint Teresa of Avila (Where the Mystical Meets the Practical)

Peers, E. Allison (Ed.). "Maxims for Her Nuns" in *Complete Works*, Vol. 3, 1963, p. 259.

Blessed Teresa of Calcutta (Pencils in God's Hand)

"Interview with Mother Teresa: A Pencil in the Hand of God". Desmond, Robert W. *Time Magazine*, December 4, 1989. Accessed March 21, 2014. http://www.time.com/time/magazine/article/0,9171,959149,00.html.

Saint Theodora Guerin (Bearing and Forbearing)

"Journals and letters of Mother Theodore Guerin, foundress of the sisters of Providence of Saint Mary-of-the-Woods, Indiana; edited with notes by Sister Mary Theodosia Mug; foreword by His Excellency, the Most Reverend Joseph E. Ritter." Providence Press, 1937. Accessed through HathiTrust.

org on March 21, 2014. http://babel.hathitrust.org/cgi/pt?id
= wu.89064865181;view = 1up;seq = 141.

Saint Thérèse of Lisieux (Small, Golden Offerings)

Paths of Love. "Letters of St. Therese to Her Sister Helene."
Accessed March 21, 2014. http://www.pathsoflove.com/pdf/
ThereseLetters.pdf.

Saint Thomas Aquinas (The Beginning of Glory in Us)

Aquinas, St. Thomas. "Expositio in Symbolum Apostolorum,
The Apostles' Creed." Translated by Joseph B. Collins, New
York, 1939. Edited and Html-formatted by Joseph Kenny,
O.P. Accessed March 21, 2014. http://dhspriory.org/thomas/
Creed.htm.

Saint Thomas More (Living the Hard Truths)

Bolt, Robert. *A Man for All Seasons*. First Vintage Interna-
tional Edition. New York: Vintage Books, Random House,
1990, p. 8.

Saint Veronica Giuliani (Seeking God's Will in All Things)

Diary IV, 272, quoted in Vatican.Va. "Benedict XVI Gen-
eral Audience, Paul VI Hall, Wednesday, 15 December
2010." Accessed March 21, 2014. http://www.vatican.va/
holy_father/benedict_xvi/audiences/2010/documents/
hf_ben-xvi_aud_20101215_en.html.

Saint Vincent de Paul (Learning from the Poor)

De Paul, Vincent (1855). "Rule of Society of St. Vincent de
Paul (1.8)." SVDPMadison.org. Accessed March 21, 2014.
http://www.svdpmadison.org/rule.htm.

Other References Used

Ellsberg, Robert. *All Saints: Daily Reflections on Saints, Prophets, and Witnesses for Our Time*. New York: Crossroad Publishing Company, 1997.

Martin, S.J., James. *My Life with the Saints*. Chicago: Loyola Press, 2006.

Swetnam, Susan H. *My Best Teachers Were Saints: What Every Educator Can Learn from the Heroes of the Church*. Chicago: Loyola Press, 2006.

REFLECTIONS AND CONTRIBUTORS INDEX